Nothing Could Have Prepared Me For This

Lynda Drysdale

Nothing Could Have Prepared Me For This

Tellwell Talent

www.tellwell.ca

ISBN
Softcover: 978-1-987985-06-1
Hardcover: 978-1-987985-07-8
eBook: 978-1-987985-08-5

Dedication:

To one of the most devoted men I know – my husband;
my supportive family; dedicated friends; and amazing
team of doctors and nurses at the Rockyview General
Hospital.

Nothing
Could Have
Prepared Me For This

Foreword:

This is a common sense look at life in general, but my own in particular.

I changed the names of the people in my life as some of my experiences with them may not have been really rewarding for either of us. Some people were innocent and some not so much.

I have experienced many challenges. I trust some of you reading this book will gain perspective on ways to approach and deal with obstacles you may be facing. That is what challenges really are, just obstacles. We simply have to figure out how to get around or past them.

I have a great support system within my family and friends but also have reached out to others in the community when I required help. Don't ever be afraid to ask for help. It doesn't mean you are weak.

You need to know where I came from in order to understand who I am. So the first few chapters are about my growing up years. My childhood was amazing! I was so very blessed to grow up with a loving family and to enjoy the freedoms afforded me by living in my farming community. I had many exciting adventures with my siblings and on my own. Some had not the best outcome, as childhood adventures sometimes do.

I kept a journal during my hospital stays and was encouraged by nurses, friends, family and clergy to tell my story. The decision to write my biography was solidified when my Independent National Sales Director with Mary Kay Cosmetics asked me to share my story with other Independent Sales Directors during a country-wide conference call.

So sit back, relax and enjoy the experiences my siblings and I had. Laugh or cry if you feel those emotions for I want you to experience some of what my journey has been.

My favorite poem:

High Flight (1937-1945)

Oh! I have slipped the surly bonds of earth

And danced the skies on laughter-silvered wings;

Sunward I've climbed, and joined the tumbling mirth

Of sun-split clouds – and done a hundred things

You have not dreamed of –wheeled and soared and swung

High in the sunlit silence. Hovering there,

I've chased the shouting wind along,

And flung my eager craft through footless halls of air,

Up, up the long, delirious, burning blue

I've topped the wind-swept heights with easy grace,

Where never lark, or even eagle flew;

And, while with silent, lifting mind I've trod

The high untrespassed sanctity of space,

PUT OUT MY HAND AND TOUCHED THE FACE OF GOD.

Pilot Officer John G Magee, Jr. (Killed in action)

I love to fly and this poem speaks to that freedom one can experience during flight.

The early years... Born in 1951, I was the eldest of six siblings, two brothers and three sisters plus a younger step-sister in later years. We lived in a quiet community in Northern Alberta on a ranch/farm five miles from the nearest town. I enjoyed the first three and one half years as an only child, basking in the limelight and love of my parents before any others came on the scene. I definitely loved my brothers and sisters. I was so excited when my brother was born and again as others arrived. My mother said I was quite taken with the baby when Norman arrived and did everything I could to help, from bringing Mom his diapers to keeping him entertained. I considered making him laugh my daily challenge. I still do this with Norman although not on a daily basis.

I spent the first several years of my life on the farm during summers, and winters we lived in a logging camp. My father was a logger to supplement the farm. Even then farming was an industry that needed subsidizing. When I say we spent the winters in the bush, I mean literally. We lived at a lumber camp miles from "civilization" with the laborers who worked there and their families. Women cooked and cared for children while the men worked cutting and gathering trees. My dad drove a Caterpillar tractor for most of our time there. Several lumber camp people ended up being part of our extended family and lifelong friends of my parents. It was obviously as good as any modern day dating internet site for matching couples, for many folk met their future spouses there.

In those early days my grandpa still owned the family farm. Dad, Mom, my brothers and I lived in a small log house in the farmyard, and when winter arrived we moved to a bush shack which consisted of two rooms. I was quite young but I still remember folks getting water from the well with buckets and my little brothers living with us in that small shack. It was a fun place to be and I gained one lifelong friend, as well as other acquaintances and friends. Those friendships remained a part of my life until after I moved away from my childhood home many years later. I renewed some of those friendships upon my return to the Peace Country in 1998.

Mom and me on a warm winter's day in the bush camp

When we were in the logging camp, we had a cat living with us for rodent control. I think he stayed there when we came back to the farm but he was a character. Mom often wore long full skirts which she made herself. (My mother was always dressed for any occasion whether it was feeding chickens or going to town and church.) The cat would cling to Mom's skirts and hitch a ride with her around the shack. We all thought it was a great game. My mother always kept a cat around to control mice whether we were in the logging camp or at home. I won't say she was afraid of mice but they have nasty habits. They are dirty little creatures. Mice urinate a path of return so they can retrace their trail. How gross is that? I really think Hansel and Gretel had a much better idea using bread crumbs. I remember Mom chasing mice with the broom. She was a pretty good aim too. When she wasn't successful, the cat took over. And there was the odd time Mom ended up standing on a chair, remembering of course, she wasn't *really* afraid of mice.

During harvest time there were threshing crews on the farm along with which came food preparations and lunch taken to men in the fields. The stooks were gathered for harvesting grain and then piled onto a horse drawn wagon. From there the stooks were taken to the threshing machine. The sheaves were then thrown into the chopper where grain was separated from the straw. For those who don't know what sheaves or stooks look like, sheaves are a bundle of grain with the stalks attached. The stalks are pulled together, tied with twine, and set on end by hand with several other sheaves to form stooks.

Stooks of grain waiting to be gathered and taken to the threshing machine

Harvesting was much more challenging in those early days with both men and women working very hard to bring crops in and put them up for the winter. Machinery was far inferior to the amazing farm equipment that is available today. Now, farmers like my brother operate huge machinery with GPS systems and every comfort you can imagine. These modern machines do everything but cook you lunch. The only time you see the old threshing machines anymore are as lawn or property ornaments. There are some folks who work to preserve our farming heritage by using horses and threshing machines to show people how harvesting was done years ago.

During harvest time women and children took lunch to the fields so men could save time. It was great fun for us! Every trip to the field was a picnic. Mother always made wonderful meals, and I remember making my grampa his iced tea. He enjoyed real iced tea. After the tea was boiled, we put it into a two quart sealer (a large jar used for canning) and then wrapped the jar with newspaper to keep it hot. Sometimes we took cold tea depending on the weather. I worshiped my grandfather, so making his tea and taking it to him was special. He was always so grateful for his tea, especially when it was made just right.

I credit my parents with giving us a rounded and full life while growing up. We were given a bounty of uncon-ditional love. We went to church on Sundays and were sent to school every day with a full lunch bucket and a kiss. There was usually fresh baking when we came home after school: fried bread scones, sticky cinnamon buns, cake or cookies. Mother regularly baked twenty-five loaves of bread every week. There is nothing quite like the smell of freshly baked bread! If you haven't enjoyed fresh homemade bread with milk or thick cream and sugar, you have missed out. Walking into the house especially on those cold days to the smells of delicious freshly baked bread in the air was just heavenly.

For many years we walked or rode our bicycles to catch the school bus one and a half miles away. At that time there wasn't gravel on the county roads. When it was wet, the bottoms of our rubber boots would build up with mud until we could barely lift them. Then one boot would lose its mud load, and we would walk lop-sided. So it would continue until we got home, first the left boot then the right. Occasionally a boot fell completely off, and we would end up with wet, muddy socks. If you were in between sizes, your boots might be just a little on the big side. Mom most often bought our boots a bit big. That way we didn't grow out of them so quickly, and of course, they could then be passed on down to the next child, so boots didn't always fit well enough to stay on when caked with mud.

On nice days, though, especially in the fall, we enjoyed walking or riding our bicycles home. It often took us much longer than it should have. However, kids will be kids and we were no exception. Many years later when

I was in Kelowna, I remember seeing a little boy who was obviously on his way to school. He was kicking a rock. Seeing him took me back in time and I thought, "This little boy is likely going to be late for school. He is enjoying kicking his rock and not in any way concerned about the time."

My siblings and friends and I often had to see who could race their bike the fastest, especially when we came to the hill near the garden on our laneway. The lane was a half mile into our farmyard from the range road. That hill seemed pretty long and high when we were children. Racing was all good until the ruts in the road caused several of us to suffer "road rash" when we hit the ground while flying pell-mell down that hill. Off those handle bars we would fly - I still have a few scars to show for it.

During the winter Dad often took us to the school bus with a cutter (horse drawn sleigh) and team of horses. We would sit on the seat next to Dad, and he would pile blankets on top to keep us warm. I still can hear the harness jingling and see our horse's breath as we drove through the snow. There were days when our weather was too cold for horses to be pulling the sleigh. Usually on those days we got to stay home. School buses would not run when it was minus forty degrees Fahrenheit. For those of you who don't do Fahrenheit, minus forty is the same in Celsius.

Snow plows in those days did not get out to the back roads often enough to remove snow. Many times vehicles could not make it through on the snow covered roads. Even after the school bus started coming a mile closer to pick us up, there were many times when Dad drove us that mile and a half with the horses and sleigh or cutter. I also remember coming home in the car with Mom and Dad on days when there had been a storm while we were away. The road was sometimes drifted in with snow. The only way we could judge where the edges were was by watching field fence posts on both sides of the road and staying in the middle. It was sometimes challenging to remain on the road. Those older cars could plow through a lot of snow though without getting stuck.

Sometimes wind caused drifting and filled ditches full with great mounds of hard-packed snow, solid enough for us to walk on. It was fun and adventurous. We never knew quite when the snow would give way and we would fall through. When the snow was hard and drifted like that, we often made snow caves. We were quite good at it although none of us became engineers or builders when we grew up. Our daughters were the ones who became engineers, perhaps because we showed them how to build snow caves, and some of our sons are pretty good carpenters.

We spent a great deal of time learning about nature. My siblings and I experienced many days in the outdoors and still do. We had pollywogs and fresh water shrimp in our lake beside the house. There was no end to life within the shallows of that lake or in the forest and grass surrounding it. Our mother always had an endless supply of living creatures in glass jars, but she never once discouraged us from our adventures. In fact, it was the exact opposite. She would provide us with jars and lids so we could capture a frog, fly, butterfly or moth, not to mention other bugs of every shape and description. She would even take a hammer and nail, punching holes in the lids for us. We were naturally curious children and learned a great deal from our environment. We spent endless hours waiting patiently for caterpillars to crawl into a jar or onto a twig so we could get them into those jars. Oddly the captured pollywogs never turned into frogs in our jars.

We knew the great love of our grandparents, aunts, uncles and twenty-four first cousins on my dad's side of the family. We all lived within about fifteen miles of one another. It has often been said of our family that we are closer to our cousins than most families are to their own brothers and sisters.

Unfortunately, except for one aunt, my mother's family lived farther away, so we didn't spend as much time with them, even though we were close in spirit. We had to take a ferry whenever we went to visit those who lived north of the Peace River, and it was always such an adventure. But it was also at least an all-day affair, and most often when I was young, we stayed overnight and came back the following day or even two days later. It was exciting crossing the mighty Peace. In the winter until the bridge was constructed, we crossed on an ice bridge.

My mother's brother, Smiley, lived on the homestead where my mom, her brothers and sisters were raised. We often stayed overnight with my uncle and aunt because of the long drive. I loved that old log home. I would imagine no end of adventures there. It seemed like a large house, but was, in fact, barely over seven hundred square feet. There were, however, ten children raised there. And, of course, there was also an old log barn with a loft. Many more adventures happened in that barn and around the farm, partly because my uncle was just an overgrown kid. He was right in on all those adventures with us. Uncle Smiley was one of our favorite uncles and still is today as I write this. He is a fun-loving, happy, gentle man, and we all learned much from him. Uncle Smiley has the greatest, warmest hugs. His wife was a school teacher, so we were expected to behave. I think it was more challenging for her to keep uncle in line. We were lucky enough to share a lot of stories and to walk and play where our mother did when she was growing up.

My mother's dad, Grandpa John, owned and operated a country store on the homestead property for many years. Although I never saw the store, I've heard many stories about Grandmother Mollie's dozens of homemade bread loaves which she baked weekly to be sold there. Our grandparents also operated the first post office in that area.

My mother told me about getting newspapers at the

family store during early homesteading years. These papers carried many stories including a series about some homesteaders from England who settled at Alice Springs in Australia. Mom was only ten years old at the time, but she was so moved by their stories that she longed to see Australia from that time on. Mom finally realized that dream when she was in her early seventies. She had the pleasure of following those early Australian settlers' well-travelled trail.

Uncle VJ, another of my mother's brothers, owned land not far from where the homestead was. He was a hunter and took two of my cousins and me to check his bear traps. All the while we travelled the trap line, he regaled us with bear stories, some of which were very frightening. He would say things like: "Once I was checking my traps on foot and got a funny tingling feeling on the back of my neck. I was pretty sure there was a bear following me, but I could never see it." Well, you can imagine three youngsters constantly looking over their shoulders from that point on until we arrived safely back at the yard. A few years later his wife, Aunty E, shot a bear at very close range when it was after her sheep. The bear had decided to take a run at her instead. She was a hero for many years, for the bear was BIG, and she had only a 410 shotgun. She took that bear down with one shot right between the eyes.

Another of mother's sisters, Aunt Ione, and her husband, Uncle Sam, owned the Market Garden at Green Island on the banks of the Peace River. The soil was rich, so corn, tomatoes and cucumbers grown there were delicious. Uncle Sam would hike with us up into the hills. When returning from those hikes, we often got cactus stuck in socks and pants because we slid down those hills on our bums. Our uncle had arrhythmia. His heart would race and beat unevenly, so when he needed to rest we could feel his pulse. He taught us how to take our own pulse. It was pretty cool although we did not understand the seriousness of his condition until he eventually died from heart complications. My aunt was a great cook, so evenings found us often enjoying a feast of corn on the cob in that old log house under gas lights and lanterns. Uncle Sam would play his mandolin while we all sang along. Those were always wonderful visits.

We also had another favorite aunt and uncle in the Okanagan whom we didn't see much. When Uncle Bill and Aunt Dodee came to the north Peace for visits, Uncle Bill would regale us with incredible stories. He was a prospector and actually found a rich copper vein that was mined and stayed productive for many years. When he and my aunt visited, I often would go hunting for fossils with Uncle Bill, looking for petrified wood or any other fossil that might peak his interest. Uncle was almost totally bald, and he told us wild stories about losing his hair when bears caught him sleeping in the mountains. Uncle Bill claimed he smoothed his hair back with honey, and the bears licked it off. He was also known for his great magic tricks with matches. He could make matches jump and start on fire. We were amazed. I'm convinced that most men in my life are just children in an adult's body.

The whole family on both Mom's and Dad's side loves music, and music surrounded us always, whether it was from the radio or Mom playing our piano. We did have a portable record player which arrived in the house when I was about ten years old. Both of my parents grew up with music in their homes, so we knew all the words to every song. Mom was always singing, and she taught us many of the songs she grew up with. Several of us also took music lessons, and can at least carry a tune. I am so grateful that she passed her love of music on to us. My dad was a great dancer, and our parents taught us to dance at a young age. We attended many country dances in the area with the youngest children coming along. It was not uncommon to see little ones sleeping on tables, under tables, or within a pile of coats in a corner of the room.

I took piano lessons to Grade seven and music theory to grade four. Our Mom had grade eleven Conservatory training and I could sit and listen to her play the piano for hours. I got bored with the type of music my teachers made me play. One teacher was a Catholic Nun and would not consider teaching any form of modern or country music. She was sure it would corrupt my young mind, and she discouraged all of her pupils from playing those kinds of music. I very much wanted to play modern music and would often sit and pick out popular tunes I'd heard on the radio just from memory. Mom was so disappointed when I said I wanted to quit piano lessons. I promised to finish the year and passed my theory with first class honors. Mom was very upset but I wanted something more than Beethoven, Chopin or Mozart. It's not that I am a music snob. I have every kind of music in my home now and did all of the time my children were growing up. My girls were surrounded by and have a great appreciation for music. I taught both of them piano basics and then paid for piano lessons later for a few years. I felt they would learn more from someone other than their stepmom.

I spent a good deal of time with my mother's sister, Aunt Evelyn, who recently passed away. I called her husband "Daddy" when I was very young. When little children smell bad, they usually need their pants changed, so I would be in quite a quandary when Uncle came in after milking time smelling like the barn. My comment was usually, "Daddy, you tink!" I expected my aunt to change his pants, I'm sure.

I fell into Uncle Daddy's milk pail once when I was two. I am not sure how it happened, but the milk was ruined for that day as I went in bum first. If you can imagine a toddler going into a milk pail bum first, it was likely a pretty funny sight. I am certain a scolding was received, but I think my aunt and uncle got a chuckle out of the incident as well. I'm sure if there had been a video, it would have made the cut for "America's Funniest Home Videos". I spent many happy fun times at this aunt and uncle's farm over the years. I was very close to my Aunt Evelyn as she had no daughters.

Their farm was located on the banks of the Beaverlodge

River. There was an amazing view and during winters we had a terrific challenging toboggan run almost to the river from the house. It was thrilling. Once you started down, there was no turning back. Bumps and humps on the run lifted us off the ground certainly adding to our adrenaline rush. When I say this run was challenging, it might be an understatement. The toboggan runs of today are wimpy compared to that one. Our biggest challenge was climbing back up that steep hill with toboggan in tow after we got to the bottom.

Of course I spent time getting into mischief with my cousin Edward when visiting there. He is three years older than I, but we had a strong bond. As a result we were co-conspirators. One time when his family came to visit ours, he and I went to the garden and picked a water pail full of fresh peas. We loved peas. We picked them to eat you understand, not for our mothers. Well we ate the whole pail, just the two of us. I'll leave it to your imagination as to where we spent the next couple of days.

My Uncle Daddy and Aunty Evelyn also always had a dog. They once owned a beautiful collie so when the television show *Lassie* was popular, Edward and I created some great adventures with their dog.

Some years later when we were teens, Edward and I went out for the evening with his friends. We had lots of time before curfew to drive to a party at the river, so off we went. On our way back, we ran out of gas miles from home. Curfew was long past due when Uncle Daddy found us. Needless to say we were in huge trouble. There were no cell phones in those days, so there was no way of contacting my aunt and uncle to tell them where we were. By the time Uncle found us, he and my aunty were both in a panic about what could have happened. My cousin left home over that incident, unfortunately, and I was sent back to my mom and dad. Having to face these four people whom I loved dearly, and dealing with their disappointment was really hard. I was too old to spank, but I remember crying buckets. We were all very upset.

I remember getting angry with my youngest stepdaughter years later when I didn't know where she was for a number of hours. I was so relieved when I finally discovered she was okay. However, I then understood why my family had been so upset when they could not find Edward and me. The anxiety of waiting and worrying sets you off. I ended up getting angry with my daughter too as many parents do depending on the circumstances. The fear and anxiety you experience as a parent causes a negative reaction sometimes. In the end everyone is emotional.

We didn't have a television at home until I was twelve, but I remember watching Saturday night hockey on our black and white with my dad. Those were the days when hockey was a great game, and players were playing for love of the game, not for millions of dollars as they do now. Those hockey nights were special times, but because of the hard hitting game it has turned into, I don't watch hockey anymore.

We were allowed only a half hour of TV after school before chores or sometimes no TV at all, depending on whether we were fighting over which show to watch or just fighting in general. With six children there tend to be skirmishes, and we only had two channels!

We knew all of our neighbors, which is not the case these days. Many of those neighbors are gone now or are very elderly. There seems to have been much more trust when I grew up and perhaps not as many boogey men. I, along with a few of my neighbors, have been trying to resurrect the old tradition of knowing and supporting your neighbors. It started sadly as a fundraiser to support a neighboring family when they lost their son to a river accident. We really pulled together and wanted to keep the closeness we formed. So there are now a group of neighbor ladies who occasionally meet for coffee, and we have also met with our neighbouring families for fun gatherings and barbeques. I also still believe that a whole community raises a child, so knowing who our neighbours are is so important.

I had the pleasure of being raised on a mixed farm with horses, cattle, pigs, chickens, cats, dogs and occasionally geese and turkeys. A goat and sheep joined our family later on and added many more adventures. We always had a dog and I became very close to a couple of them.

My father planted grain so we enjoyed the bounty of a grain and hay harvest. Our gardens were always full of vegetables. There were lots of potatoes and thus they warranted a separate garden. One of my sisters-in-law years later said my mother was a great example for *Better Homes and Gardens*. We also grew fruits such as rhubarb, strawberries and raspberries.

We picked berries in the summer and put up preserves,

canning many fruits and vegetables. I remember filling a boiler tub full of saskatoons in about four hours of picking one day. Mom would usually can about one hundred jars of saskatoon berries for the winter. Once when my youngest sister, Tish, was a baby, Mom had me stay close to the truck to watch baby while she picked berries. Mom probably felt she could be more productive in the picking department than a twelve year old, which I was at the time. As usual she was right. I had my baby sister in my arms and was picking some raspberries. As luck would have it, I stumbled into a hornet's nest. What a commotion that raised. I was running screaming for Mom and protecting my baby sister. While I was protecting her, though, nothing was protecting my butt. Many stings later Mom stripped me down and sat me in a mud puddle. It did work, but I was mortified, not to mention sore. I couldn't sit for days.

There were raspberries and strawberries to preserve as jams and jellies. Mom also made her own sauerkraut, another form of stinkiness, in the basement. She covered the cabbage with a strong salt brine in a ceramic croc. Mom then put a board with a rock on it atop the cabbage to hold said cabbage down in the brine. There it would brew until the cabbage became sauerkraut.

Putting up the preserves and picking berries was a great bonding time with our mother. We couldn't avoid talking and sharing. Many years later even my brothers would call and say; "Mom, we need to talk." Of course there were some things you just didn't share with your mom, just because she was your mom. It still isn't cool to tell your mom everything!

We grew the most awesome rhubarb. It always tasted best raw and dipped in sugar. It was not unusual to see several children with little plastic cups containing sugar sucking on or chewing a piece of rhubarb while walking around our farmyard.

We had a vegetable bin in the basement which consisted partially of dirt walls where we kept our fresh vegetables over the winter. It was like a cold room so vegetables didn't begin to spoil until late winter or early spring. Our cat, Patty, caught a weasel there once and what resulted was a huge battle. The cat did win although that is unusual. Weasels are a formidable opponent when backed into a corner, but he met his match in our old cat, who by the way lived to be nineteen years old.

Our mother also canned chicken and moose meat which helped us through the winter. Dad supplemented our diets with moose, deer or elk in the fall. Our parents butchered them on the farm along with our other meat animals: cattle, pigs and fowl. This may gross a few of you out, but it was a matter of fact in those days. Farmers had to self-sufficient. I didn't like the larger animals being killed even though it was done humanely. I did, however, enjoy cleaning the insides out of chickens. There were almost always eggs developing, some that were ready to be laid or nearly so. Even if the shell was not fully formed we could still use those eggs. Sometimes we found amazing items too, and I looked at this chore as a treasure hunt. Chickens will eat the darndest things. They are much like magpies and crows when it comes to shiny objects.

It was awfully scary when the time came to kill the chickens. Dad used a sharp axe so it was quick, almost like using a guillotine. You may have heard the phrase, "running around like a chicken with its head cut off." They actually did run around with their heads cut off. It freaked me out! There were children scattering whenever those chickens ran, so you can imagine my dismay when I heard the "Headless Horseman" story.

Mom sold eggs and cream for extra money to help pay the bills. We separated cream from the milk and put it into special five gallon cans. We would then take those full cream cans into the dairy processor in town about thirteen miles away. When I was older and because I did the milking, some of the cream income was given to me. I'll bet you didn't know there are fifty-one pieces to a cream separator. Of course most of you wouldn't, but when it came time to clean all of those pieces, they had to be put back in exactly the right order. If you didn't get the order of the parts just right, there would be milk spilling everywhere. At least the discs were numbered. Mom and Dad got a little twisted when it came to wasting food, so when the separator started spewing milk it wasn't pretty. Usually it was me that caught heck.

We made our own butter, and children were in charge of beating the cream in a big crock until it formed butter. Once when Mom went to town, she left us to finish making the butter. We have a great picture of my brother Johnny hamming it up wearing only his underwear and a towel while he performed some pagan dance around the churn. There was cream everywhere, but it was mostly churned to butter when Mom arrived. We had the ability to make most tasks fun! There were enough of us so someone always had a great idea, and I'm pretty sure we tried every one.

My mom always said there was room for any people that showed up at mealtimes, and very often we had extra folks. It might be a neighbor, a school friend, an extra farm hand, just about anybody, so we simply added another potato to the pot. Our family still carries on that tradition. People are always welcome at our tables.

We had no freezer for many years, so meat was kept on ice in the pump house during winter and even part of the summer. We lived by a lake and were able to get plenty of ice during the winter. It was great when we finally acquired a freezer – less work for everyone. Mom was ecstatic!

We used a ringer washer for doing laundry. I remember getting the baby diapers wound all around the ringers and calling my mother in a panic for help. I hated washing the baby diapers. We used scalding hot water, so I had a special stick to scoop the diapers from the water and put them through the ringers. The ringers were two tubes, similar to rolling pins, which spun toward each other. You would put the diaper between the ringers and the machine would do the rest. That process wrung out most of the water. The trick was to get just the right amount of diaper going through the wringers at the same time. We then hung the clothes outside to dry and ironed them with a gas iron once they were dry. Our ironing board folded into the kitchen wall, which saved on space.

Mom cooked on an old wood stove for many years until we upgraded to propane. She entered her baking at the County Fair every year and won first prize for her Angel Food cake many times. With the new propane stove, Mom just couldn't get those cakes perfect as she had before. I remember after six tries, she actually cried because she took such pride in her Angel cakes. She finally mastered the new stove and was once again Queen of the Angel Food cakes.

As we got older, all of us entered the County Fair with different projects. I liked the animals, so the task of showing a Shetland mare for a friend of my father's one year quite naturally fell to me. A Shetland is a smaller horse. At this particular time the mare had a young filly by her side and even though baby was close to the show ring, the mare was so upset at the separation that I was pummeled by her sharp hooves almost the entire time we were showing. I think the judges took pity on me for we won first prize that day. The mare was a nice little horse other than being spoiled and agitated about her baby. I also took first prize with my Appaloosa filly in the halter class two years in a row.

4-H was a wonderful experience for all of us. What a great way to develop public speaking skills, learn responsibility for an animal's health and well-being, and become proficient at record keeping. We learned how to school a one thousand pound calf. Sometimes the calf won and dragged us around for a while. There was the odd time when the calf had to be led with the tractor until he figured out how to follow a rope. Our projects varied, but mostly we worked with cattle. I raised a beef calf with the highest rate of gain one year. He was a big boy but gentle as a kitten. I cried for days after the sale. Instead of "Charlie" I should have named him "Steak" like one of my nieces did. She had a daily reminder not to get too attached because inevitably he would be food in somebody's freezer.

My dad's brother George, convinced me to join the 4-H Dairy club, and I enjoyed my Holstein cows more than the beef calves because we kept them on the farm.

They didn't have to be slaughtered. I taught Josie, one of my milking projects, to let me ride her. The other cows would follow us when I went to bring them in for milking. The odd time I ended up on the ground when Josie didn't feel like coming to the barnyard or was just being cantankerous and bucked me off.

We were raised in a great old two-story house with two bedrooms on the second floor. Mom and Dad had one bedroom and the children the other until our family grew too large. We were also getting older, and privacy was becoming an issue. There was no attic so two closets were removed from under the eaves in the children's room and that one was split in two. Those closets had been a great place for adventures. They were long, running the whole length of the wall, so provided lots of places to hide and use your imagination. Once the renovations were complete, the boys had one bedroom with the girls sharing bedroom number two. The littlest child slept in a crib in Mom and Dad's room.

I really loved that old house. It had so much character. There was a sun porch on the south side where I could often be found on a warm summer day. It was a great place for a nap. I had a satin blanket and teddy bear for those occasions.

As we got older it wasn't uncommon for us to sneak out onto the roof of the sun porch from Mom and Dad's bedroom. Once when my youngest brother Johnny was being chased, he threatened to jump off that sunporch roof if our brother Norman came closer. Of course Norman didn't take Johnny seriously. Well, jump Johnny did. Good thing he was a nimble little guy because he came away pretty much unscathed.

Ross Lake Farm: Our playground where we learned so much about life while growing up

Our house was heated with a big old coal/wood furnace in the basement. Mom got up early and stoked the furnace so we had heat going through the house. Shoveling coal was not much fun as it was dusty and dirty. It was a necessity, though, and we had to make sure there was enough coal in the coal bin which was located in the cellar. Once mom got the furnace wound up, we would come downstairs and dress by the heat registers. The linoleum floors were pretty cold, particularly during winter. It was mighty chilly some nights, and we had tanned moose hides on our beds to keep us warm. I have always loved the smell of tanned leather, and that is likely one of the reasons why.

Mom also made us moccasins from moose hides. She sewed most of our clothes, many times making her own patterns. We had hand-me-downs from our cousins too, so we were never without nice clothes. Not all of my siblings would agree with the "nice" part as hand-me-downs got pretty old and ragged for a few of them. They would have preferred new store bought clothes. Mom made each of my sisters and I matching dresses a couple of times. She also fashioned and sewed suits for my brothers from old coats. She was an excellent seamstress and went on to make our grad gowns and wedding dresses, doing a beautiful job with each.

I recall an incident in later years when Mom was doing

some custom sewing for a lady. This lady had requested a gold lame gown for an award evening at the local theatre. Once the dress was completed, Mom asked her customer to come for a final fitting. Once the dress was on, Mom became concerned that it was too form fitting and underwear lines would be an issue. Mom was politely informed by the lady that she would not be wearing any underwear. Mom was speechless as the dress was cut down to here and up to there and left little to the imagination. I would have loved to have been a fly on the wall when that conversation took place. My mom is not particularly old-fashioned, but I know she was properly shocked that day.

Our telephone was an old-fashioned wooden box that hung on the wall. We were on a party line, and each neighbour had a different ring with a series of long and short rings. Our ring consisted of four longs. There was one lady on our party line who listened in on everyone's conversations. Whenever she was listening, we would say outrageous things that would get her tongue wagging. We would have half the neighbourhood pregnant, drinking excessively, or fighting. She would then broadcast the information to everyone she knew. It was fun to shock folks with our crazy stories.

Because there was no indoor plumbing, we had to use an outhouse. It was a small wooden building very often with a permeating odor and sometimes without toilet paper. There was a "catalogue" on hand just in case that happened because it was too far to run back to the house and get more paper. On occasion, that outhouse was more than a little chilly for parts that should not feel that cold. Later Dad put a pail in the basement with a toilet seat on it, and of course the pail needed to be emptied frequently - not the most pleasant bathroom situation but better than having to run outdoors in the winter when it was cold.

We went to church on Sundays most weeks and wore our Sunday best clothes. Dad and my brothers would sometimes figure ways to get out of going, but usually we all went together. We had great summer picnics with the church group, which included most of the community at that time. I'll never forget the little English bachelor who always sat in the back pew snoring to his heart's content. Shorty had an excellent singing voice, but often during the sermon he would drift off. When church was over, he would shower the minister with praise for such a wonderful sermon. It always amazed me how someone could sleep through church - not to say it wasn't boring on occasion. My cousin Jenny and I would make up little verses or words to go after hymn names and get the giggles while sitting through the sermon. (eg."Jesus loves me ... under the bed.")

When we were older and no longer in Sunday school, we joined Hi-C, a young people's church group. Everyone had a great time as our minister was a very forward thinking person. He actually took us to different churches so we could see how other people worshipped God. I think he was rather wise as most of us stayed with our own church, partly because of that experience, I'm sure.

We built a new house on our farm when I was going into grade twelve. We had three indoor flushers. WOW! Real toilets! What a treat!

Another great thing about the new house was having a bath and shower. Before that we shared an aluminum bathtub usually on Saturday nights. I didn't mind that so much except as I got older there was not much privacy. And I did mind when little ones peed in the water before it was my turn in the tub.

The last one always had to empty the tub as well, which

meant scooping enough water out, pot by pot, until the tub could be lifted to the sink and poured out. Dad did fix up a shower for us in the basement of our old house when I was in my teens. It was cold and quite crude but we thought it was the best thing ever!

More about my personal growing up...I was a kind and loving child but rather precocious, curious and adventuresome at the same time.

My mother tells a few stories about times I was too young to remember. For instance the day I went walking with my border collie, Bingo, and we met up with a groundhog. I spent hours with the dogs and cats. Bingo, our farm collie, was my babysitter when I was little. He would herd me to a safe place if he thought I was in danger. It was he who kept me safe when confronted by the groundhog.

Just at the walking stage and my shoes had holes in them — an indication of how my life would unfold?

Hanging out with my teddy and little red wagon; notice the teddy has only one eye. He was well loved.

I was only two at the time, and Mom noticed what was going on in the barnyard. The groundhog was confronted by Bingo. I am sure I would have been going to check out that ground hog when Bingo took control of the situation. Mom rushed to the dog's aid, broom in hand. Bingo was already swinging that groundhog around his head when Mom arrived. This was just one of the many times my poor mother was frightened about my well-being.

I learned to ride cows and horses at a very young age. Before I could walk my dad put me on the back of a quiet old Hereford bull named Trump. This bull tipped the scales at fifteen hundred pounds, but he was amazingly gentle. I remember Dad doctoring Trump's feet. Dad put an antiseptic mix in boots made out of tire inner tubes. After Trump's boots were on his feet they were tied on with sisal rope or binder twine. The liquid in the boots sloshed some when he walked, but Trump took it in stride. It was a funny sight, a bull wearing boots.

I graduated to horses later on and would do anything to get outside and go riding. My chores done, I would hop on a horse and go for a ride, especially on nice days.

And it was a great way to get out of doing the dishes.

You all know, I'm sure, that there is nothing more gratifying to a child than running through warm wet mud! When I was two years old, my mother had me dressed up for an outing. She told me not to get my new shoes dirty while she got ready. Well, you can guess what's coming, right? Mom found me going for a walk in the mud. When confronted, I quickly sat down, in the mud and told Mom, "I keen it off Mommy." Mom snapped a picture. I must have been pretty serious about "keening" off my shoes as Mom had to go to the house for the camera. There were no cell phones then, remember?

Another time my best friend Ann and I were going to town with our mothers. We were probably four years old at the time. It had rained but was nice and warm, and there were, of course, puddles. The two of us were outside waiting for our mothers. We were wearing cute little dresses, all pretty and ready for our trip to town. Are you getting the picture? That mud was just too much invitation. Needless to say our moms were beyond consolation when they saw their little angels. I daresay we were in trouble again. However, our moms kept their sense of humour long enough to take pictures of us before the scolding began.

Everyone has a friend during each stage of life. Only the lucky ones have the same friend for all stages of life. My muddy friend, Ann, and I are forever friends and I feel so blessed to have her!

Sitting in the mud cleaning my new shoes ("I keen it off Mommy")

With my muddy friend Ann

My childhood pal Poncho

Some years later when I was about twelve Poncho became my sidekick. He was a beautiful dog, a pretty Collie cross, caramel in color. He was an all-around special mutt. We travelled together everywhere around the farm whether I was hiding out from doing the dishes or going for a horseback ride. We also spent hours on the lake banks, exploring or just hanging out.

Poncho and I hunted mice one time because I felt the cats needed food. There were about fifteen of them around the barn so off we went in search of mice. There were bale stooks in the field. A bale stook is similar to the stooks of sheaves for threshing but square bales are actually rectangular and were stacked horizontally ten to fifteen bales to a pile. The stooks look similar to pyramids.

Poncho and I were merciless. We tore those bale stooks apart and found a whole pail full of mice. I moved the bales. Poncho would kill the mice in one bite. What a hunting team we made. My partner and I took our bounty back to the barn. The cats refused to consider the fare we provided, simply turning tail and sauntering off. We were not amused as it took us the better part of an afternoon to fill that pail and there were many bales not in stooks anymore, which my father noticed quite promptly. Needless to say we had to go back out to the field and stack those bales again. We were feeling very dejected and unappreciated all the way around.

I've always loved kittens and cats and have rarely been without one in my life. I taught barn kittens to line up in a row behind the milk cow. I then squirted the milk from the cow's teats toward their faces. They became pretty good at catching it, but if Dad walked into the barn when this was taking place, I was in trouble for wasting milk.

Helping do outside chores gave me a chance to be with the horses and also avoid doing housework, which I detest to this day. I didn't even mind so much milking the cows before school except when the cow smacked me with her tail, which was most often not so clean, or when she kicked and stuck her foot in the bucket. It was even worse when the cow kicked the bucket over. I always got into so much trouble when the cow was really to blame. I tried all sorts of ways to keep those cows from kicking. We used "kickers", a short chain with a curved piece of metal on each end that hooked around the leg of the cow just above the mid joint of her leg. This apparatus was supposed to keep the cow's legs in place so she couldn't kick. Hah!! There was one cow in particular that was a master at getting her foot into the pail with "kickers" on. I also tried tying their tails to an overhead beam. That seemed to make them just that much more determined to put their foot in the pail. I guess I appreciate why they wanted to kick. If you had cold hands placed on your nether regions and pulling on you when your udder was full of milk you might kick too.

Milk was a source of income and food for the table as well as a requirement for our human babies, not just calves. There were a few days when I went to school smelling a bit like cows, but that is just the "smell of money" as my brother Johnny puts it. Besides, we were raised in a farming community, and I wasn't the only one in our rural school who had to do chores before catching the school bus.

One of the less pleasant jobs on a farm was cleaning the barns. Dad made a manure boat from a grain elevator belt. It measured about four feet across and was about six feet long. He attached a single tree which is a board with chains on it to be hooked to the horse's harness. After we used a pitchfork to load the manure, we hooked the manure boat to the harness of our work horse, Dan. Out to the manure pile we would go, turn Dan around, walk him back over the manure boat, tipping it upside down in the process, and thereby unload the manure. Slick, in every sense of the word!

But, the chicken house... well that is another story. If cleaning barns was unpleasant, cleaning the chicken house was torture. Chicken manure makes your eyes water. It stinks! Baby chicks are really cute but they grow up to be chickens, and they then become gross and smelly, although somewhat strange and interesting creatures, especially a pet chicken we had called Penny. She was slightly crippled, so when Penny felt in danger from the rooster or another hen, she ran to one of us and jumped into our arms for protection. It was quite a performance!

Chickens roost at night and are very easy to catch when they are sleeping. My brother Johnny and his buddy moved some roosting chickens into the neighbor's car one time on a Halloween night. Guess what the car looked like next morning. The boys were found out and had to clean the car. I don't think my brother's favorite birds are chickens either.

Speaking of Halloween, it was a common thing for youngsters to go out trick or treating. When we were young, Mom dressed us in cute costumes and drove us to the neighbors, where we were given popcorn balls, candied apples or homemade fudge. When we were older, the tricking started. We would do crazy things like put straw bales on the farmer's door step, turn the power off at the power pole, put toilet paper around the yard, or put syrup on the door handles of cars and then skidaddle before we were caught. Tricking ended for some of us one Halloween night when one of the less hospitable neighbours came from his house shotgun in hand. When bullets started whistling through the trees above our heads, we made for home in a hurry.

Occasionally a neighbour's cow would end up wearing a saddle, or a hay wagon would be on top of someone's barn. Those pranks I didn't get involved in, but they did create some interesting situations. Turning over outhouses was also a popular prank, and ours was no exception. There was the odd story around about the owner of an outhouse moving it just a couple of feet from its foundation before the tricksters got there. The joke (as well as less pleasant things) was on them when they fell in the hole. There were some people who threw rotten eggs or did things that were destructive, but for the most part everyone just had fun on Halloween.

I became quite a tomboy because I was six years without a sister. My brothers and I had some great adventures. Johnny and I once tried to convince Norman to jump off the roof of the barn. We were at the age when flying seemed like a novel idea and something we should try. We found a sheet and leaped off the pig barn into a bale stack about six feet below. Of course, the sheet would not open far enough so in our minds we needed more height to give us the right conditions for parachuting. The barn it had to be. We had nearly convinced Norman to jump when he chickened out - which was a good thing. It was definitely a recipe for disaster. I'm not sure if Norman is still afraid of heights, but chances of that are pretty good.

Dad had built a big flat deck wagon with airplane tires on it, which he used to haul hay bales. There were just two tires so if we all ran to one end the wagon would tip up. One of us would stay there while the other two of us ran back to the other end. It had the same effect as a huge teeter-totter. It would toss one up in the air a few feet when the other two of us ran to the other end. Dad wasn't really pleased when he found out what we were doing with the wagon. Norman broke his arm falling off that wagon. He broke a few bones while going through those discovering and adventuresome years.

The farm was an awesome place to play hide and seek too. It was a game we could play for hours. We constructed a play house in the trees, and one of the granaries was an incredible theatre. We wrote, acted and produced our own plays.

There was a rod that supported and strengthened the walls of our barn when it was filled with hay. This literally kept the barn from "bulging at the seams". The rod was an amazing tightrope although you did not want to be straddling the bar if you fell. My brothers may have fallen victim to the crotch catch a few times.

The neighbors had a rope in their barn loft and we played trapeze stunts there. If we hung on and swung just right, we could swing all the way from one side of the loft to the other. We had to be careful though not to let go over one of the holes in the floor. There were openings along the outside edges of the loft where hay was thrown down into mangers below.

We played outside games of Tag, Hide and Seek, Simon Says, Anti-I-Over, Scrub-when there were enough kids to play it – and, of course, Cowboys and Indians. In the winter we made snow angels as well as played Fox and Goose. We also skated and made snow forts. We constructed some pretty elaborate forts when there was lots of snow and the conditions were right.

When it was too cold or late to go outside, we often played card games like Fish, Crazy Eights, Rummy or Whist. And there was Scrabble but the boys didn't like to play word games as much as Chinese Checkers.

One time when my parents took us to visit Ann's mom and dad, she and I decided we would eliminate the tent caterpillar population. They were especially bad that year, so we took pails into the pasture and proceeded to pour gallons of water on the caterpillars. We now know had we added a little dish soap or salt to our water the project would have been far more successful. All we did do however was get very wet, much to the chagrin of our poor mothers. At least we weren't too muddy that time.

When I was about ten years old, we had a hired man who was like a big brother to me. One day Dad asked the two of us to bring in a load of bales. The hired man drove out to the field, and then I took over driving the tractor while he threw bales onto the wagon and stacked them. Everything went really well until we were on our way home. I was still driving and we had to cross a bank to get back on the lane. I didn't negotiate that ditch very well, and disaster struck. The wagon tipped to one side and the entire load of bales slipped off including said hired man. I learned a few new words that day, bad ones I shouldn't ever repeat. But it was pretty funny even though we had to reload all those bales. Needless to say the hired hand was mad at me for a long time.

Our Cowboys and Indians adventures were played out in the bushes around our yard and cow pasture. The stories we could have made into movies were plentiful, especially when we got old enough to be riding without supervision. We jumped off the pig barn onto horses' backs just like the Lone Ranger and Zorro. We even taught a couple of our horses to lower their heads so we could hang onto their necks and let them throw us up onto their backs. We eventually even jumped on from behind the horses like cowboys did in the movies. I think we all tried Roman Standing on the backs of two horses at the same time. Often you could see one or the other of us standing on a horse's back just for fun while it was trotting off in some direction.

Tree climbing was another one of our specialties. We could shinny up a tree pretty fast and were often found sitting on a branch. Johnny was pretending to be Tarzan one day, swinging from branch to branch in the poplar trees. He was doing pretty well until a branch broke, and with the Tarzan yell turning into a scream, he came crashing down, breaking his arm in the process. Although it was an adventure gone wrong, we can laugh about it now. It was kind of funny at the time too, if truth be known (well, maybe not for Johnny.)

There was a big birch tree on the east side of our lake which was fun to climb. I remember getting pretty high up and having a branch break. Fortunately for me there were lots of branches and I didn't meet with the same fate Johnny had in his Tarzan incident. I did get some nasty scrapes but escaped without more serious damage.

Dad giving me a ride on the mayrath

We had a garden tractor called a mayrath. It normally

had a motor between the two front wheels. Dad needed the motor for his grain auger, so the mayrath was no longer motorized. We children pushed it around the yard. One of us had to steer, so we always argued about who that would be. Once when friends were over, six of us pushed that mayrath down the lane and up the famous garden hill. When we got to the top - because it was so hard to push up there in the first place - we decided all of us should climb on to ride down. Johnny ended up sitting between the two front wheels. He was one of the smallest, and we couldn't all fit so that worked well, or so we thought. Wouldn't you know, we hit a rut on the lane going down that hill and off popped Johnny. Thump, thump, under the wheels he went. We likely hurt him but threatened him with serious injury should he tell. It took him a bit to catch his breath, and then he cried. We felt bad then but that was just another incident that Mom and Dad did not uncover until many years later when we were regaling them with childhood stories around the kitchen table.

The lake was a source of adventure as well. We were often found at the water's edge, much to our mother's dismay, mostly because she could not swim and neither could we. There were blood suckers (leeches) in it, but there were also many other wonderful creatures. We had beavers a few times. There were lots of muskrats, and there were always swans in the spring. My brothers took a raft out to see how close they could get to the swans one time. Bear in mind that swans have a wing span of about six feet and my brothers were all of eight and nine years old on a makeshift raft, and couldn't yet swim. Needless to say it was a close encounter of the frightening, feathered kind.

And then there came a great adventure in the lake with my brothers and me. I would guess that many of you who are reading this book do not know what a pig trough is. Well, my father built one for our pigs to eat from. It was probably six feet long and made from rough cut lumber. There were three heavy planks making up the sides and bottom of the trough. Wooden rungs were then attached to separate the pigs from eating each other's food. It was similar to a canoe but looked much like a hollowed out log with rungs. In the infinite wisdom that children often have, we decided it would make a **great** canoe. So we pushed the trough down to the water's edge and prepared to launch. Being the oldest, I was persuaded to go first. I wedged my body between the rungs so I was sitting flat on the bottom of our "canoe." We didn't have a paddle. The idea was that my brothers would push the "canoe" away from the water's edge and hand me a stick.

Unfortunately, the lake still had a little ice around the edges, so our shore line was anything but even. As my brothers pushed this "canoe" into the lake, the corner of our craft caught some ice and neatly flipped with yours truly within. Remember I was wedged in and now my brothers could not get the "canoe" to stop rotating. I was flipped upside down three times before they were able to get the trough to stop turning. Although we were a little scared after it happened, we have spent many a time recounting this story over the years with much laughter and maybe a little embellishment.

After the boys got me out of the water, we scooted up to the house. They created a diversion, and I sneaked up to my room. I changed out of my sopping wet clothes and left them literally in a puddle. Mom asked the next day where the water leaking out from under the closet door came from. Of course we didn't know. This was another story that finally came out around the kitchen table some years later.

Perhaps one of the most unusual incidents involving

our *inland* lake occurred when Mom saved a pelican that was stranded in the ice one fall. He was *way* off course and got stuck as the lake was already partially frozen over. The ice was thin enough that Mom laid some boards out across the ice. She then crawled on her stomach to retrieve the bird without falling through. Remember my mom could not swim. She nursed that pelican for a few days in our basement trying to save the poor thing, but he succumbed to his ordeal and was subsequently stuffed and given to the local museum.

During the winters there were times when our lake would freeze over with no snow on top of the ice. When that happened, the ice was smooth as glass and covered the entire lake. We could skate the whole way around, close to a mile in total. It was incredible fun until there was a loud crack or whoomping sound as the ice moved and shifted under our weight. Even though there was no danger of falling through, that noise would scare our pants off.

We had a horse fall through the ice one time though. Gypsy was her name. She came too close to a muskrat house and the ice wouldn't hold her. Dad, our hired man, and a neighbor hauled her out with ropes and the tractor. She was in a sling in the barn for a while as she ended up with pneumonia. Awhile later that same horse had an unfortunate experience while in training. At that time she belonged to our hired man, and he had tied her to a post which was lying on the ground. Gypsy pulled back on the rope and the post moved. When a horse is scared, it's either fight or flight. The log moving frightened the little mare and she *flew*. She went through barbed wire fencing at least twice. The veterinarian did a fabulous job of stitching her up with well over two hundred stitches to her chest. She survived that experience and went on to overcome yet another life threatening situation when she ate too much grain. When a horse eats too much grain, it will founder. The gut cannot process the grain and a blockage results that a horse cannot get rid of. Although the condition is often fatal, Gypsy did not die and continued to live a healthy life for several more years.

A few years after our hired man trained Gypsy, I got to call her mine. She then had a beautiful Appaloosa foal. I named that filly "Queen of Bathsheba" or Sheba for short. She is the horse I showed at the County Fair. We took first place for two years in a row in the halter class. I spent many years with that horse. A few years after marrying my first husband, we hauled Sheba in the back of a pickup from Dad's farm to an acreage not far from where I lived in the city. I was then able to get away from the hustle and bustle and enjoy leisure time with my old friend. She lived to be twenty years old, and I missed her badly when she was gone. She taught my stepdaughters and several other children a great deal about riding horses.

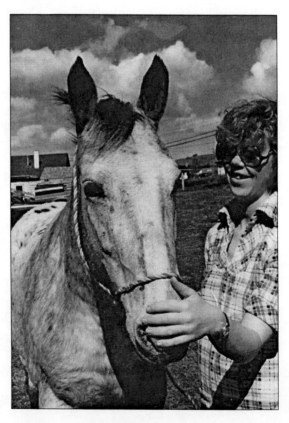

My faithful horse Sheba

I recall one time when our eldest daughter wanted in the worst way to saddle Sheba by herself. She was an independent child and resisted my tightening the cinch (a strap toward the front of the saddle.) This strap basically anchors the saddle to the horse. I let Cassandra put the saddle on by herself, and needless to say, the cinch was not tight enough. As she and her friend rounded a corner, I could see the saddle start to slip. Both children were sitting in the saddle as it quickly flipped upside down beneath the horse. Sheba tried to inch herself under the saddle as it was falling off but to no avail. The horse stopped immediately, turned her head, and with a look of total disgust, waited patiently for the crying children to get up and out from beneath her. The majority of horses would flee in such a situation with children and saddle flying around under them. What could have been another riding disaster became a funny tale because the mare was so gentle and not easily frightened. She was what we call pretty much kid-proof.

I had the pleasure of riding a number of different horses while growing up. We learned to ride on the work team, a couple of Clydesdales called Bell and Dan. They were the most gentle of animals, and I remember we had six children on Bell's back once, just to see how many of us could fit at the same time. It was a long way to the ground as we soon found out. One child started to slide off and held tight to the one in front. It was a domino effect, and…another broken arm resulted, my brother Norman again.

Horses have been a huge part of my life thanks to my dad and mom. I used to hurry through the milking to go riding. I could tell my horses and dog all my troubles and never have to worry about them sharing my secrets. Sometimes just saying things out loud makes concerns seem so much smaller.

One time a neighbor friend, Ally, and I became the girls in a commercial we had seen on television. There were two girls with long blonde hair running their horses through a field. The grass was up to the horses' bellies and the girls' hair was flying in the wind. Well, we both had horses and our hair was long and blonde. We didn't have any grassy fields that tall, so we chose Ally's father's wheat field. There we were, two blonde girls re-enacting the commercial, galloping through the wheat field with our long hair flying out behind us.

We knocked down a great deal of grain that day and

our fun resulted in a serious reprimand. Needless to say that incident set the record for trouble that year. We definitely got "grounded" in the most basic sense of the word. And that was when "grounded" wasn't even a word used by parents. We weren't allowed to ride our horses for about two weeks.

The two of us also used to night ride and were often out until well after dark in the summer. We had good reliable steeds, but our parents did worry when we didn't show up by midnight. There was a half mile where we had to ride solo in opposite directions to get home. Of course there weren't any "bad guys," but every shadow or bird flying in the night was enough to send us scurrying home. I'm sure we set some speed records and were actually lucky that neither of us had a fall during those dangerous night rides.

My father and a long-time friend went into the ranching business together when I was about ten years old. They leased a large tract of land about eighty miles or approximately 130 kilometers from our farm. About May 15th we would haul the cattle to the ranch with cattle liners and bring them back on or close to October 15th. When the cattle were there, we went every two weeks to check on the herd. It was usually fun as we camped: sleeping in a tent, riding during the day, making river crossings, and finding all sorts of interesting situations. The riding wasn't so pleasant when it was raining and cold. One time Dad pretended to be a bear outside of our tent and scared the heck out of us. We thought we were doomed!

One thing Dad always told us about bears – "The only predictable thing about a bear is that it's unpredictable." A lesson I learned well, and I have the greatest respect for bears to this day.

One time while most of my family went to the ranch, my cousin Jenny and I were left home to do chores. On our first night alone we had an amazing thunder storm. We weren't supposed to have the television on during thunder storms, but being teenagers we had talked ourselves into it. We were watching a suspense movie. On our farm we always had a menagerie of pets, and at that particular time there was Pepper, a cute little goat. He was afraid of the storm too, but he picked the worst time to try to come into the house. At a rather scary part of the show and just when there was a loud crack of thunder, he chose to jump onto the window sill behind us. You can imagine our fright when we turned and saw his face peering in the window. We both screamed! I think that scared the little guy more than any thunder he heard that day. It was also the last time he ever jumped up onto the window ledge and the only time we watched a scary movie during a thunder storm.

When I was about five years old my grandparents moved to town. Grampa James still visited the farm nearly every day. I dearly loved my grandfather and was in total awe of him. He was a big man, tall and robust with a strong presence. He was firm but had a very soft heart. He carried Juicy Fruit gum in his pocket for the grandchildren and had generous warm hugs for us. Grannie Glendora was a pioneer school teacher and could be judgmental at times but always believed children are the future of the world. She was definitely the matriarch of our family.

Occasionally, I stayed with Grannie and Grampa in town. I remember their house being small with only three rooms. My Aunty M, Dad's oldest sister, gave Grannie a light that had Niagara Falls on it. Whenever the light was turned on, it gave the illusion of the water actually tumbling down. There was also a gas furnace in the living room that made noise when it came on. Between the furnace and the coo-coo clock I woke up every hour, as they were sounds I wasn't used to hearing on the farm. When the train was passing through town, we could feel the whole house shake as the track was only a block away. And of course the whistle would blow as the train made its way through town, another startlingly unfamiliar sound.

My Grannie Glendora made the best brown bread in the country, or at least we thought so. The smell when she was cooking it was wonderful, and in later years she wrote down a basic recipe that each of us has to this day.

I wrote a poem for my Grannie Glendora that I was able to read to her before she passed away many years later.

"Grandma"

As a child I took you for granted

Seemed like you were always there when I wanted.

Christmases, Easter, a birthday too,

Yet I never really thought about you.

I remember the old English couch well

And your fresh baked brown bread had such a delicious smell.

All of your ornaments and trips around the world

Seemed like fantasy when I was just a little girl.

My scholastic and musical achievements

Were highly praised by you,

But I treated your suggestions with resentment

And my mother's too.

When I graduated, I started to realize

That you were right to criticize

The many foolish things that I did.

Now I treasure my memories of you during my childhood.

I'm glad that I can express my gratitude and love

Before you've met our maker up above

I am told in many ways and actions I resemble you.

Well, Grandma, you just don't know how proud I am that I do.

And, someday, when you are gone, I will remember.

To you Grannie with all my love.

I also remember pictures of my great-grandparents on the wall of Grannie's home. I used to stand and look at them trying to imagine who they really were and what it would have been like to live in those times. I sometimes felt misplaced, that I ought to have been born a century earlier and longed to have known them in their youth. They were early pioneers in the Clover Bar district near Edmonton, Alberta.

My Aunty M took over as matriarch of the family probably in part due to her military background. Aunty M was a nurse for the United States Air Force and spent a good deal of time travelling to and working in various parts of the world. She brought us presents from the countries she visited. I still have a porcelain doll from Mexico as well as a Hummel figurine from Germany. The Hummel is a baby's face on one side of a porcelain ring. The baby is watching a bumblebee on the other side. I did not know the value of that little piece until sometime after I married. I felt the figurine needed cleaning so took a brush and soapy water to it. When I turned it over I nearly dropped it. I knew by then what a Hummel was and that it certainly had more than sentimental value. It now rests in a special but safe location in my home. I also received a beautiful housecoat from my aunt one time, which I wore for many years. I may still have one or two cleaning rags left from it. Aunt M had great stories to tell about her grand adventures. She is now, at the age of ninety-two, still living on an acreage with her Yorkshire terrier. She maintains a large garden with assistance as well as her flowers and yard.

I admire her courage and her fight to maintain independence. She is losing her sight but still manages to keep her place in the country. Aunty M now depends on others to help get around as it is not safe for her to drive anymore.

Those of you who have enjoyed the privilege of growing up on a farm will appreciate what I wrote a few years after I had moved to the city:

"A Farm Morning"

The sun lifts its sleepy head, and crawls onto the horizon.

Yawning its brilliant colors across the sky.

The lake, calm and cool, lies quietly mirroring its surroundings.

The trees stand motionless against their picturesque
background.

A rooster suddenly breaks the silence with a piercing voice,
announcing the awakening morn.

In no time, it seems the entire farm is stirring with deliberate
movement.

An occasional twitter is heard as the birds begin their daily
routine.

The cattle drift slowly in the direction of the barn and their
morning feed.

A young colt romps toward his mother to suckle her special
milk.

The dog stretches and barks at an imaginary menace as the
shadow of a hawk slips silently by.

The dependable farmer emerges from the still, quiet farmhouse
into the clear, fresh morning.

He walks with long strides to the barn with the dog close at his
heels and is greeted by the babble of gossiping hens.

The morning blossoms like a flower slowly unfolding.

School Years... Now I know some of you are going to think "yeah, the good old days," but they were. We walked one and one half miles on dirt roads for some years to catch the school bus.

There were thirteen students who were in the same grade from grades one to twelve. A number of our student group never left the area, and since I moved back, we see each other now and again. We also have regular high school reunions.

I had an awesome teacher in grade one. She was like a grandma to all of us, and, in fact, was the real grandmother to one of our classmates. That wonderful lady taught all of the children in our family except for my youngest sister and step-sister.

In grade two we had a teacher who had the greatest floor mat. There was a town painted on it with streets and everything. Being a tomboy, I thought it was pretty wonderful, for we could play with cars and trucks on the mat. We also could bring our dolls to school so I had the best of both worlds.

Grade three brought another wonderful teacher to us. She had lost her husband at an early age. She remarried during the year she taught us. She wore her wedding dress to school one day so we could see how beautiful she was on her wedding day. She looked like a princess in her soft blue organza. There were layers and layers of dress, and we were so impressed. She also thought of us as her kids and still visits me occasionally. She and her husband own a small farm only a few miles from where I currently ranch.

In grade four we had a rather stern teacher who was the mother to one of our classmates. I remember the excitement we created during a particular recess. There were several of us who had detention and weren't allowed to go outside to play. Our teacher had to ring her bell to call the other children in. We waited with bated breath. *Somehow* a grasshopper was trapped under her bell, and it made a giant leap as soon as she lifted that bell. It was quite hilarious to those of us who were in the room - except for the teacher, of course. We pranksters ended up staying in for more recesses due to that episode.

My Grandmother Glendora and my Aunt Ella had occasion to substitute as teachers in our classes. I remember having a difficult time remembering to call them "Mrs." instead of Aunty and Grannie. Aunt Ella was my dad's oldest brother's wife.

In Grade five my teacher taught me to cure the hiccups. All you do is hold your breath and take nineteen swallows of water without taking another breath in between. It works every single time.

Grade six we were in a portable away from the rest of the school. By this time our school had outgrown itself, and we were stuck out there by ourselves. One afternoon my teacher wouldn't believe I had to go to the washroom until it was too late. I still cringe with embarrassment when I remember that I didn't make it to the school bathroom in time.

Wouldn't you know it – that teacher followed us into grade seven. She was very good at her job and we did like her even though she was such a stern teacher. She also was the part-time librarian, so we couldn't get away from her no matter what.

Grade eight saw us with a young and fun teacher just out of university, but she left partway through the year to get married.

Grade nine we were with an older teacher and of course still full of shenanigans. We had to see what would happen when we put a tack on the seat of her chair. We got a lecture over that one. "A person could get really sick with a prick from an unclean pin". So then we decided to put a mouse in her desk drawer. That didn't turn out to be as funny as we had hoped either. She had an amazing way of making us feel very bad. In hindsight she could have had a coronary when she opened that desk drawer. Then we really would have been sorry!

Then came high school. The first thing that happened to us there was "Initiation." We had to be slaves for the Grade eleven and twelves and dress up in the weirdest costumes. It was embarrassing but fun at the same time. I guess these days it would be considered a form of hazing and a totally unacceptable practice.

There were a variety of teachers in high school, some better than others.

Dating…I didn't date much and mostly hung out with a group of kids. We were all friends with some more close than others. There were a few girls who had steady boyfriends and some small cliques. But because we were a farm community, it was not that bad. Actually today we hug our classmates when we meet them somewhere and sometimes have coffee or lunch to catch up on each other's lives. Students that were in other classes are still friendly too. That is one of the great things about growing up in a smaller community and school.

My first two dates were rather disappointing. I went out with a guy from summer camp. We went to a show with his sister and her boyfriend. I was shy and also very innocent. As it turned out, all four of us had to sit in the cab of the boyfriend's truck. There were no club or crew cabs in those days. Four of us on the seat of the truck necessitated our sitting very close, and I was so humiliated. It was a horrible experience as I couldn't relax. I sat stiff as a board the whole time, so needless to say we didn't go out again. Another time I dated a fellow whose family owned a bakery in town. I don't even recall how I met him, but he was a very handsome young man and drove a hot car. We went to a movie with his brother and his brother's girlfriend. When he tried to run over a cat just showing off with his fancy car, I asked him to take me home and never saw him again either.

Our group of friends had a great deal of fun, and we did so much together. When I was in grade eleven and twelve, I attempted the dating scene once more. There was a neighbor boy who was older than I by a few years who wanted to get serious. I wasn't anywhere close to that. I remember having a hard time breaking it off because I felt sorry for him. First cardinal rule of dating is, "don't feel sorry for the guy if you don't want to be with him." And so I broke his and a few more hearts.

One summer I went to a camp sponsored by the United Farmers of Alberta. We stayed in cabins, the girls and boys being separated of course. *Somehow* one evening there happened to be a great deal of debris covering the chimney of the boy's cabin. Therefore the smoke did not go up and out of the cabin. The next morning I found myself in the boys' shower, sleeping bag and all. Being the totally "innocent" young woman I was, the boys "mistakenly" decided I had been in on the mischief that sent them scurrying from their cabin while it filled with smoke.

We had a great time at camp. There were a lot of shenanigans but all were innocent fun, and no one got into any real trouble.

These happy memories are very different from what young people often experience today. There is a country song about how no one died doing the things we used to do. The song speaks of how sad it is that now there are school shootings. Violence seems to be so accepted by too many people today. So many young folk have come to accept horrid events as the norm. Is this the influence of television, video games, and movies?? My thoughts are yes, this is so. There are far too many reality shows, crime series, and violent video games. Sometimes when you turn on the telly there are only horror movies, reality shows and crime series. What happened to *Little House on the Prairies?* With video games the bad guys always come back another day. In real life when he dies, he really is gone, not ever coming back…

My first serious challenge…Although my early years were innocent and carefree, I too experienced the unexpected violence in our world. When I was seventeen, I was raped by a guy I thought was a friend. I was easy to lure away from the group because I didn't suspect a thing. We hiked up a big hill away from the rest of our friends. He made it sound exciting and challenging and I was always up for a challenge. I was a fun loving kid and always had friends around me. I thought nothing of going along with him. When we got to a secluded area, he grabbed me. At first I thought it was all in fun and he wanted to wrestle. I was a pretty good wrestler but was no match for him. He was hurting me and told me not to scream. I had once seen him pick up a car, so I knew his strength. I didn't scream as I was very afraid, but I did fight him.

I was understandably distraught and embarrassed. I felt violated and very alone. I had never been threatened before especially by someone I knew. I also had no real self defense training to fend someone off in a situation like this. I was so afraid of him afterward. He said, "Do not to tell anyone or awful things will happen." I believed him. He was fairly popular simply because he was a bully, so I never told a soul.

In 1968 unless there was a witness, women and girls

had no chance of proving rape. There was no DNA evidence back then. "No" didn't necessarily mean no, and I didn't have any visible marks to indicate an attack. Thank goodness I didn't get pregnant. The fear of that possibility had me in tears more than once until I was certain there was no pregnancy.

I was so afraid no one would believe me and that my father would do something drastic that could have sent my dad to jail. From that point on I never allowed myself to be cornered with no way out.

Many years later I took a self defense course with a policeman who recognized my fear and helped me work through it. Since that time I have truly dealt with the rape, had some very good relationships with men, and finally forgiven the perpetrator. He committed suicide many years later, and I've often wondered how many other victims there were. I have felt guilty occasionally for not having stepped forward, but the fear of doing so kept me from saying anything. I knew reporting this crime would have been an awful experience without a satisfactory outcome. Who would have believed a naive innocent teenager coming forward after the fact without hard evidence?

After that experience I was pretty cautious. I went out with the crowd and very rarely by myself with any guy. Those I did hang out with were fellows I was very comfortable with. I made sure I had a way out or that things never went far enough to put me in danger. For many years I didn't trust men. If anyone held onto me even in fun I would get very uncomfortable and sometimes feel panicky. I only dated young men who were unsure of themselves and afraid of my dad. I made sure they were also guys who respected me.

I would encourage any woman to take self defense training. The only person you can truly rely on to protect you in a situation such as this is yourself. I sadly learned that everyone cannot be trusted. I definitely lost my innocence in every way when the rape occurred.

I had a couple of fellows ask me to marry them, but I wasn't ready and intuitively knew they weren't the right man. I ended those relationships when they got serious. Over time I had and still do have many male friends. I find relating to men on some levels easier than women probably because cattiness and drama are traits I dislike. Sometimes women take hold of an issue and never let it go. Ladies, take responsibility for your actions.

So many women carry baggage for years and years. It just isn't worth it! How many do you know for instance who blame their mothers or fathers for things they cannot control in their lives, stuff that happened years before? We have to take responsibility for our own actions and the lives we live. Once you are an adult you make your own choices, and most know the difference between right and wrong.

Don't blame your parents for what goes wrong in your life. And unfortunately relationships do crash. Having a pity party is okay and you may need some time to heal, but don't draw everyone else into your drama. After a while no one wants to hear it.

Having said this, I must also say women are strong creatures. God made us that way. We often carry the weight of our family's troubles and our own but continue to support our family, our friends, and whoever else needs our help. A strong woman is pretty much unstoppable especially if she has the support of those around her, most importantly, her partner or significant other.

Life with my first husband... When talking about the strength of women, I am reminded of my first marriage.

I went to work at a local store after high school while waiting to enter the nursing program. There I met my first husband, Mark. He was an assistant manager and wore a suit to work every day. Most men I knew only wore suits to church, weddings and funerals. Otherwise, it was jeans, sweatshirts or clothing to wear on the farm. Despite his more formal appearance, Mark was a fun-loving guy.

Now let me tell you, ladies – some of us have to be married once to find out who we shouldn't marry.

Despite the unsuitability of my first husband, I did have fun and learned a lot about being married. The day of my wedding I was standing in the vestibule of the church with my bridesmaid, Charlie. She told me not to go through with the wedding. Charlie said, "I'll hold the door. You don't have to do this." She and I had both witnessed some things in this man for the two weeks prior to our wedding that just didn't impress either of us. It is a good idea to make sure you are with your fiancé around family, your old friends, your mutual friends, and children for some time before you say yes. He wasn't very nice to my family, especially my youngest sister. Tish was having a hard time, as I spent several years helping to raise her and she missed me when I moved out. Mark didn't think she should be clinging to her big sister and told her so quite rudely.

So getting back to the girl holding the door at the church; I said to Charlie, "I care about him. I can make anything work, and besides look at all of these people in the church. I just couldn't do that to my family or his!" I then went ahead and did it - to me, to us! I married him for better or worse.

I had the opportunity to go through some old letters recently while I was de-cluttering and found Mark's "love letters". He had been transferred to another city before we married, and I was left behind. In the letters Mark never asked about me or my family but certainly told me how tired and over-worked he was. Never were there expressions of undying love for the girl he was to marry. Oh, he said he missed me but it was for purely selfish reasons.

Our first home together was a basement suite. I was nursing and Mark was an assistant store manager. We moved to a rental house shortly after and ought to have purchased that home. There was a suite in the basement with a great tenant, and Mark's father wanted to lend us the down payment. The tenants rent would have paid our mortgage, but Mark was not a risk taker, so we didn't buy the house. The property today would be valued at approximately twenty times the original price of twenty-eight thousand dollars. The vision of hindsight is 20/20, wouldn't you agree?

Mark was transferred to Kelowna for a short time where I worked part time for an insurance agency. After five months, just long enough to meet his friends and make some of my own, we were on the move again to Nanaimo, where we stayed for about one year.

Mark left his job then, and we moved to Victoria, where my mother's wonderful brother-in-law, Joe, hired Mark and provided him with an excellent opportunity. I became employed by another retail chain and was advised there would be no considerations for any promotions due to the fact my husband worked for the opposition.

I left their employ and found a job at the public auto insurance company. After being on strike, I had an opportunity to move up in the company, and Mark had been wanting to change careers, so I transferred back to Kelowna, where he had grown up. My employer paid for our move. Mark then went to school while I worked and paid the bills. I didn't mind so much when Mark was taking his schooling, but in between courses when he was not employed, it was difficult. Mark once told some friends in my presence that his television and his wife were working, so why should he? Not a good thing to say when the bill payer is there. Needless to say life for him over the next short while was not much fun.

After a few years we were on strike again at my work place, so I worked three jobs to pay the bills, while Mark was either in school or looking for work. Maybe I shouldn't be so hard on him, but that was a time in my life when his support was needed, and I was doing **all** the supporting. He did pick fruit some to help out and worked a few jobs, but he still expected me to pick up after him and make the mortgage payments.

I finally had had enough. Mark wasn't working again, and I suggested we seek counseling as things were spiraling out of control. That didn't go well. Mark did attend one counseling session with me, but soon after it was as though we had never been there. He didn't think *we* had a problem; in his opinion, it was *my* problem. Mark said he was quite happy.

After he had been out of work for several months, I told Mark to leave and find work. I said, "Once you show me you can be responsible, find a job and work for a while, then maybe we can work things out." Mark left town and moved back to Calgary, where we had started our life together. He worked for a friend of ours refinishing old pianos. Mark bought me a beautiful piano probably hoping to regain my favour. It is a lovely piece of furniture. Our friend, Doug, had found the piano (painted green) in an old church in Chicago. Doug had wanted me to have a piano for some time, so he likely encouraged Mark to buy it for me.

I had that piano for about two years before Doug was killed in a plane crash on his way to a remote location. The pilot was flying him to a lake resort where he was to enjoy a fishing trip he'd won. Doug was a very special guy so it was a shock and he was sadly missed by his family and friends.

I remember flying to his funeral and thinking a plane crash wouldn't be such a bad way to leave this world. It was a day much like the one on which he died. The skies were beautiful, almost ethereal.

I kept my piano for many years and treasured it until arthritis forced me to give up playing. One of my nephews now has it for his children, who are taking piano lessons.

Mark was working away when I finally realized our marriage was truly over. I had every suspicion he was being unfaithful. I received a credit card bill with a charge for flowers, and Mark had told me years before the only way he would ever buy me roses was if I bore him a son. *He actually told me that.* Because of medical complications in my early twenties, I couldn't have children, so receiving flowers from him was not going to happen. As a result, I always grew my own. After receiving the bill, I called him, asked him who had received the flowers and what she had done to receive them; then I told him I was finished. I actually didn't give him a chance to explain. I don't think I really wanted to know, and I still don't care.

He admitted to having a female roommate and once told me my only competition would be a blonde woman with green eyes. He assured me this relationship with the roommate was totally platonic. I naively believed him, although in the end I had every reason to believe otherwise.

At this point I would have to say that a marriage is two sided, and we all contribute to the success or failure of relationships. I was not one to openly challenge my ex-husband and when faced with an unhappy situation, I usually kept my own counsel. Perhaps had I been more vocal about my feelings, pressing him when things were bad, it may have turned out differently.

I also know that most people can be challenging at times, and I'm no exception. I wasn't an angel and certainly gave him some grief as well. The sad thing is Mark would not accept the fact we needed help in saving our marriage, and I waited too long before insisting that he take some responsibility.

I do know it would have been difficult to save our relationship no matter what help we received, so we got a divorce.

Adventures with my ex-husband... I must say I had some good times with Mark too.

Once during a beautiful fall day, while Mark and I were exploring some back country with friends, we discovered an old log cabin. We had taken four by four trucks as far as we could and then hiked the rest of the way. The area near Harrison Lake is beautiful and remote with considerable logging activity. The roads are treacherous and just a bit scary. When we hiked in to the cabin, we found a hot spring. The spring emptied into a large Olympic size log swimming pool. The pool was murky so we chose not to jump in, but there was an old claw foot bath tub and the hot spring water was running through it. Ahhhh!... that tub was heaven sent! We all took turns soaking our sore muscles as we had walked several miles to find this place.

Mark and I spent many great times with friends we gathered from the different places we lived during our time together. Mark and I were both athletic so we played many sports together. I learned to snow ski, as well as water ski. I played softball, watched many ball games, did lots of camping, cycled, partied, and went exploring the back country with friends and our four by fours. I didn't care for racket ball because Mark hit the ball harder, and many times I came away with bruises.

Some of the funnier moments we experienced together occurred when we were water skiing. Do NOT wear a bikini when water skiing. Although I was mortified at the time, the incident was hilarious in retrospect. Bikini bottoms will come off if you hit the water hard enough when falling. I was able to catch those bikini bottoms on the end of my toe, but could not get them back on without drowning, so I had to crawl into the boat *au naturale*.

I also recall camping at a lake next to the train tracks. About three o'clock in the morning a train came through, whistle blowing. Well, it was every man for himself, never mind the women and children. I laughed so hard I was crying. If you've never seen a grown man leap from his sleeping bag, stand up in a small pup tent and try to find the opening while still half asleep, with a look of sheer terror on his face, let me tell you they should make a movie. That experience likely took ten years from Mark's life.

Another time we were on a ski weekend in Washington. We had a radar detector because Mark had a bit of a lead foot. (I did too, truth be known). Anyway, we came around a corner and there, low and behold, was the state trooper. He pulled us over and asked how fast we were going. Mark said he didn't know for sure. The trooper said "Well, son, I clocked you at sixty miles an hour and braking hard." It was a fifty mile per hour zone. My ex got a ticket for speeding. I guess you had to be there in order to appreciate the trooper's dry sense of humour, but I had a difficult time not laughing out loud. He was intimidating for sure. When he came up to the car, all you could see was his belt buckle.

A great friend of ours had the habit of catching Mark off guard, and once she and I dropped in to visit him at the store where he worked. Mark, who was not expecting us, was standing on a ladder about the second rung from the floor. Our friend sneaked up behind him and ran her hand up the inside of Mark's pant leg, asking him if she could give him a hand. He nearly flew off the ladder. We chuckled about that for a long while.

When I was learning to snow ski, Mark and his friends took me to a small mountain close to where we lived. I had never been on downhill skis. Riding cross country skis behind a horse is totally different, let me tell you.

You stop when the horse stops, but on downhill skis you have to turn to stop.

We picked up our rental skis and went to the top of the hill. The tow rope was a real challenge. I fell off and slid part way down the hill. Up I got and when we finally arrived at the top, Mark and his friends left, telling me they would come back. I was left to my own devices. I was pretty angry and frustrated when a couple of young boys came along. One of them laughingly said the fateful words, "I'll bet she walks down!" I already had my skis off and was quite prepared to do just that. Needless to say I received just the motivation needed to make me don those skis again and start downhill. Remember I said you need to turn and stop? Not me! I went straight down that hill and right into the snow fence. Fortunately no one was killed in the process.

The next time Mark and I went skiing we were at a much bigger mountain. Again I was left on my own. This time there was an instructor teaching a class just ahead of me, so I tagged along just far enough back that I didn't have to pay for his lessons. I refused to be daunted into accepting failure.

After I had learned how to ski, Mark and I were on

a ski lift one time with our friends. Doug was just a few chairs behind us. It was bitterly cold (-32 degrees Fahrenheit) and the chairlift suddenly came to an abrupt halt. There was dead silence. We were thirty feet off the ground with no escape from the biting cold.

From the chair behind us came Doug's booming voice, "This is the Lord speaking! Mark, you have been evil!" Needless to say the moment of tension was over as we burst into laughter. Everyone on the chairlift was laughing so hard the chairs were bouncing up and down, which was a little unsettling for some of those more "height-frightened" folks.

I grew up while I was with this man though – I had to. Mark had a great many good points and I still care about what happens to him, but being with Mark is not the place for me. His mother agrees with me. She and I have remained friends all these years. I admire this mother-in-law for her wisdom, strength and warmth. She is still a mother to me and has actually apologized, saying she didn't raise Mark very well. After our divorce, Mark's parents and I used to meet secretly for coffee because he had threatened me about having any contact with his family. Despite the difficulties I had with Mark, I still love his family.

I gained many friends during my first marriage and some very special family, but I do believe things happen for a reason.

My love of downhill skiing... One of the great things about being married to Mark was that he introduced me to downhill skiing, which soon became one of my passions. I spent eight years as a Canadian Ski Patroller while we lived in the Okanagan. I became proficient at the sport and loved it immensely.

I need to expound a little on my adventures with the Ski Patrol. Some days it was cold and miserable at the mountain, but we had to be there making sure everyone was okay and picking up the ones that weren't. The good days more than made up for those cold days.

I enjoyed the people that were a part of the ski patrol system. Some were absolutely nuts, but most were just a whole lot of fun. Free skiing was a bonus, but most of the members were ski patrollers for the right reasons, helping people who were injured. We dealt with some ugly injuries and situations. I think one of the worst was a fiftyish gentleman who had a heart attack on the lift, and we were not able to save him.

Skiing at the hill where I spent most of my time as a ski patroller

Another incident that immediately comes to mind was attended by a wonderful ski patroller, a young man by the name of Francois. He had come from Quebec with a desire to learn better English, make new friends, and have the opportunity to ski at some wonderful resorts.

Francois trained with the rest of our patrollers that year and was very proficient with his first aid even though he struggled with his English. He failed his first written exam simply because of that difficulty with our language. We offered to retest him in French. Francois refused and wanted to re-write in English. We contacted our Board and were able to give him another English test. I was well aware that he knew his course inside and out, so we were thrilled when Francois passed the second exam.

On the particular day I wanted to tell you about, Francois was the lone patroller at the mountain as weather conditions were lousy and no one wanted to ski. One of the maintenance crew was servicing a bull wheel at the top of the Bunny Hill. The bull wheel pulls a cable up the mountain with the lift seats, or T's, attached to it. It was a perfect opportunity for the work to be done as there was literally no one there. It just so happened a couple of skiers arrived and wanted to ski.

The manager started the lift. Normally the lift would be locked out during any type of maintenance, but for some reason, the lift started and the young man who was working on it was caught up in the machinery. His right leg was severed, and the left was chewed like hamburger before the lift could be stopped. Francois attended to the victim using all of his skills. The paramedics and doctors who attended that difficult grue-some scene were actually sick to their stomachs, but Francois maintained control until it was all over, and incredibly saved that young man's life.

The accident victim went on to live a useful and pro-ductive life with his one partially salvaged leg: getting married, raising a family, and having a successful career.

We unfortunately lost our dear Francois a few months later when he contracted meningitis. It was a terrible loss. He was so brave, with such a promising future, and far too young to leave us.

Francois was recognized for his bravery at our National Symposium with his family in attendance. He will be forever remembered.

While with the patrol I had the opportunity to do some traveling, not just to other ski hills, but to competitions and symposiums in Montreal, Quebec, and Vancouver. I was a member of the National Board of the Canadian Ski Patrol System for a time and helped organize the symposium in Vancouver. There were usually five hun-dred or so patrollers and members of the ski system who attended these yearly functions, so there was considerable work in the planning of such an event. Flying to Vancouver for monthly meetings with a local patroller who was working toward his pilot's license was a bonus. He needed the hours so flew us to Vancouver once a month while we were preparing for the symposium. Our pilot went on to become a successful commercial pilot.

Some skiing adventures…The cliff at the mountain we patrolled was not open for public skiing. Part of our job was to control the build-up of snow thereby excluding possibilities for avalanches. We learned a great deal about snow layers, how they developed, the various conditions that produced them, and what took place with shifting of those layers under certain conditions. We also learned to use dynamite. The cornices had to be blown up in order to keep the mountain safe.

To the right side of the ski resort was a cliff which was out of bounds, but the patrollers would ski there when it was safe to do so. I remember my first time down. I was a "powder hound" and used to search out the great powder snow. The other patrollers told me to ski about two-thirds of the way down and then straight run it from there. There was a lake at the bottom, and you needed to have enough speed to get partway across, or you had to walk for about a half mile, which is difficult at best on downhill skis. I did what I was told, whooping it up all the way, except that I turned downhill too soon. I came off a knoll at enough speed to send me about twenty feet into the air. I landed in a cloud of snow and came out the other side, amazingly still on my skis. What a rush!

There were a few funny tumbles that left people around me laughing merrily. Once I was patrolling the Bunny Hill. For those of you who do not ski this is the easiest run on a ski hill designed for children and those just learning. I was "shushing" along showing off, making quick little turns. Suddenly my skis caught an edge. Two other patrollers were on the lift going up and witnessed my fall, a complete blow-out! There were toque, gloves, ski poles and me all over the hill. Nothing was hurt except for my pride, especially when one of the patrollers called out, "Good job, Lyn! Were you testing your bindings?"

Another tumble I will share with you was a dandy. We had ski patrol competitions once on a bizarre run called the Gun Barrel. This run is narrow and almost straight up and down. Our slalom course was set up and we were to complete a relay race with the first aid toboggans. There were sand bags in the toboggans to give realistic weights and conditions. Thank goodness we would never have taken an injured person down a hill with the break neck speed we did that day. At any rate I almost made it to my hand off before I crashed. It looked pretty spectacular to the onlookers, so I was told. Again, I came up unscathed, other than some bruises, with my equipment and the toboggan spread all over that hill. And because of the steepness of that run, debris was spread over some distance. A trip to the chiropractor had me right as rain again.

Skiers are known for having fun and we sure did. There were lots of parties and many great memories. Two poems I wrote during this time illustrate not only the fun we had but also my love of skiing.

When you have a passion for what ski hills offer, you may think something like this as you drive up to the mountain.

"Lesson in Humility"

There it is, rising, seemingly from nowhere.

A royal panorama, breathtakingly beautiful in the morning sunshine.

I hurriedly ready myself for the heady pleasure the mountain promises.

Then civilized complexity prevails as I am herded toward the only mode of transportation upward.

Scooped up by a mechanical hand, I sail rapidly into the air, several feet above the fluffy white snow.

The sky-borne seat sways slightly as a stiff breath of fresh mountain air passes by.

I turn and look backward at the endless panorama etched and painted there.

All too soon, realism pulls me back from my reverie and I disembark.

Downward I glide, skimming a packed trail with great anticipation, attempting to meet the challenge facing me.

In a matter of moments I am forced to stop and recuperate, breathless, but confident.

Adventuring forth, I begin skirting tall snow-laden pine trees.

Suddenly I am surrounded by and floating through pillows of soft white deep powder, a skier's dream.

Then the inevitable mistake on a perfect run sends me tumbling headlong into the godly white blanket beneath me.

Laughing uncontrollably at my plight, I turn to face the
mountain. It belittles my mirth, taunting me.
All at once I realize I shall never conquer any jagged expanse of
nature's perfection.
I can only enjoy the attempt at her convenience.

On a snowy day in the Okanagan, February 7, 1981,
when members of the ski patrol zone were in a funk,
we decided to do something crazy. A birthday was celebrated, experiences on the mountain were shared, stories and jokes were told, spirits were lifted, and a new
spark was instilled in our patrol.

"Untitled"

No snow?

Moral low?

Zone 4 – Pacific South Division

Have found a solution!

A descent of eighty or more steps – be careful, don't spill the
brew!

Twisting, turning, down we go – beginning to get a clue?

Laughter and merriment filter from below,

Now we can see a flickering glow.

At once we find the scene is set.

This may be the best party yet.

A campfire surrounded by friends,

Just then the music ends.

Somebody cuts loose with the "Rodeo" song.

And everybody starts singing along.

The lake slaps the sand.

A friend you haven't seen in a while shakes your hand.

I started to smirk.

Who really thought it would work?

A beach party in the dead of winter.

Surely you can't be serious!

One thing I never had the opportunity to do was helicopter skiing. That line on my bucket list will unfortunately never be crossed off. At this time in my life I am unable to do any type of skiing. You will understand why later in my book.

If you have never skied, take a lesson or two. I do recommend it. Skiing is exhilarating, challenging, and fun! It is a sport that you do for yourself. Take your time if you wish, do it at your own speed. Whether you become a great skier or not does not matter as long as you enjoy the experience, and sharing your fun with friends makes each skiing day a special memory!

So I will tell you next about some more of the fun things I've done…Having been an athlete all of my life, it was natural that I would enjoy bike riding. Now I don't mean just casual bike riding. I am talking about getting on a ten or twelve speed bicycle and pedaling your brains out. Of course, I never did anything by half measures anyway. So I started riding my bike around town and got serious about staying in shape for snow skiing. In the morning I would ride my bike four miles to the pool, swim laps for half an hour, and then ride another four blocks to work.

After work it was all uphill going home. A number of times I would arrive at my house and just fall under the water sprinkler. I don't "glow' like delicate women, I "sweat" like a man. So by the time I got home on a hot summer day, I was drenched, red in the face, and panting from the exertion and the heat. The cold water was decidedly wonderful and definitely cooled me off. This practice could have given me a heart attack with the sudden change in temperature, but I was strong and healthy.

I had formed a friendship with a gal through skiing, and we decided a bike tour adventure would be great.

Dot lived in another city so I'm not sure whose idea it was, but we agreed on the route and dates. So these two *corporate* employees, one of whom had never been camping before, decided to rough it in the Rocky Mountains and ride from Jasper to Banff, a distance of about one hundred and twenty miles (190 kilometers), all mountainous terrain. We both rode bikes and skied several times per week in the winter, so we were in excellent condition. I also swam nearly every day. You talk about six pack abs and being buff! I do wish I could say my body was in that kind of shape today.

I decided to play a little joke on Dot. In those days there was no such thing as bear mace. If you encountered a fur ball in the woods, you pretty much turned tail and ran. I convinced my friend to try to locate some bear mace. I told her there was none to be found in my town. Dot diligently searched sporting goods stores until some kind soul put her out of her misery and said there was no such thing.

Needless to say, I got a telephone call that night. We had a good chuckle over it. She was pretty gullible but also had a good sense of humour. When Dot came to join me, we loaded up our bikes in the pickup, and

Mark drove us to another city to catch the train. The train station is about a two-hour drive, so he was a good sport about taking us there. It was very early in the morning to boot. We caught the train at five A.M. and were on our way. The train ride was a delightful scenic trip through the mountains, and we enjoyed visiting for several hours.

After poking around the town of Jasper, we decided to find a camping spot and just chill out for the evening. To our dismay the camp grounds were full, so we had to ride farther down the highway in hopes we would locate a campground before nightfall. We rode for several miles and came upon a beautiful camping area at Athabasca Falls. Fortunately, there were just a few spots left, and we acquired one for the night. We pitched our tent and ate supper.

We then met some of our neighbors, people who were also cycling but headed in the opposite direction. There was a couple and their single male friend. Both of the guys were in the Armed Service. I really liked the single guy (we can call Hank just for fun.) I have no idea where he is now. We hit it off and went for a long walk sharing many stories, but I was married at the time and was not about to two-time my husband, so that's where it stopped. Hank was a great guy, and in another life we likely would have spent more time together. He was an outdoor enthusiast and physically fit. He also loved to ski so we had a great deal in common. I've always believed things happen for a reason so there must be a reason we didn't "happen."

I had schooled Dot about wildlife we may encounter, and one of the rules was to place all food in a lock-up. We carried our food in our bicycle saddle bags, so after storing our food in the lock-up we returned to the tent. Some other people in the next campsite cooked hot dogs over their open campfire and fatty drippings fell into the fire pit. Needless to say, late in the night there arrived a bear. He (or she) sniffed around that campfire pit and ate whatever charred remains there was of the hot dogs.

When Dot heard the bear, she sat straight up in her sleeping bag and with a fearful voice whispered, "Lyn, there's a bear, there's a bear!" I told her to lie back down and remain very quiet. I said it would go away. The bear was only after the fat in the fire pit. I believe that Dot is an expert at holding her breath; I really don't think she breathed until that bear left.

Sometime later though, probably about three o'clock in the morning, a second bear arrived and started sniffing around our tent. Dot was fast asleep, having finally drifted off only moments before, as I'm sure she was still scared to death. I lay listening to the bear thinking, *Why would he be sniffing around out tent?* Neither of us wore any perfumes and we used baking powder for deodorant, so there would be no odor. Then it occurred to me… we had applied a muscle liniment to our aching bodies before going to bed. *Oh dear!* I still managed to lie very quietly until the bear moved on. I did not wake Dot. I figured if the bear started to make a move on our tent, I could get her out of there pretty quickly and yell for the army guys we had met to bring a weapon. I knew my girlfriend wouldn't waste any time scrambling to safety; however, she slept through it all, and the bear moved on without incident.

That morning we were up, had our breakfast, and got on down the road. We had many miles to cover before the end of day. The paved road into the campground backtracked about half to three-quarters of a mile, and we could see the highway across a big open meadow.

We decided to cross that meadow as the crow flies.

The ground was rough so we had to push our bicycles instead of riding them. There were a number of vehicles stopped alongside the highway and people were watching something. Sure enough a brown bear (cinnamon bear to some) was ambling across the meadow.

Dot panicked and started to run with her bike while screaming, "There's honey in my saddlebags!" It was quite a sight! She was hot footing it across the meadow, saddlebags flapping and bike dipping and diving in every direction, but she was still moving forward.

It was obvious the bear was heading for an open garbage bin at the other side of said meadow, so the tiny container of honey would not have been detected by him in a million decades. I was doubled over laughing so hard that if the bear had really been hungry, I would have been lunch I'm sure. Many of the folk watching the whole spectacle were entertained by my poor friend that day.

A couple of days later we arrived at the beautiful Peto Lake, an aquamarine jewel situated in a pristine mountain valley, unequaled in beauty.

There was a log cabin which doubled as a store and tourist information center. I was out of film, so went to purchase more. Dot had spied a young bull moose and wanted to take some pictures. As I rode away I said, "Please be careful. Don't get too close."

I had never known Dot to laugh in the face of danger but that day she heeded me not. Maybe it had something to do with the bear mace trick I pulled on her. At any rate when I returned, she was very excited, saying she was within just a few feet of this creature to take his picture. When I admonished her for being so foolish, she only said, "Well, there was a guy with some really expensive photo equipment who went nearly right up to the moose. I thought if he wasn't concerned about his equipment, I should be okay."

I then asked her if she would crawl into a pasture full of cattle because the bulls would be "tame." Her indignant reply was, "Of course not!" I said, "For goodness sake, you were looking danger right in the face. A moose is NOT a domestic animal but a very wild bull in his own environment! Please don't do anything like that again!" She did, however, get a great picture of the bull-moose. He subsequently went on to be a famous moose. He was aptly named "Easton" and has his mug shot in many photo albums around the world.

Cycling through the Rocky Mountains

The rest of our trip was eventful as well. We met several other cyclists. We considered them a bunch of pansies pretty much. They rode fancy bicycles which cost too much money. Most of these riders likely spent time in a gym but not anywhere else. Okay, I'm being judgmental, but their equipment consisted of cameras … and a *van*. The van would stop to pick up stragglers, who would ride in comfort rather than work at cycling. Their gear was stored on the luggage rack atop the van, and we were informed their tents were erected, and everything was prepared and waiting for them at intermittent stops. They even had *steak*! NICE!! I wonder what they had to pay for all this luxury.

On the other hand, here were the two of us gals with our not-so-expensive ten speed bikes. I rigged mine with two lower gears so I had just a little more "go" on the really big "grunt" hills. We also packed all of our luggage, tent, repair kit, extra bike parts, and food with us on our bikes.

We each likely had about sixty pounds added to our own body weight pushing up the hills. We made our own meager meals and erected our sleeping quarters, aka, tent. We also bathed in the very cold and icy mountain streams. Let me tell you that was an experience in itself. When the water is freezing your hair, you know it's cold. Our dunkings were brief although we jumped in every day to remove the sweat and refresh ourselves.

We used baking powder in our personal regions to avoid chaffing and absorb moisture. It is very effective but can be irritating if not removed daily. Baking powder is similar to flour if it becomes wet, just to give you some perspective.

Our next adventure took place when I lost my brakes going down a hill. Now, I say hill lightly. We are talking about the Rocky Mountains. This hill was approximately four to five miles long. When I realized there was no way of slowing down I was travelling about forty to forty-five miles per hour. That speed is not so bad if you know you will come to a stop and don't have to turn any corners. Well, wouldn't you know it? There was a corner at the bottom of the "hill." I was continuing to gain speed. Now a ten speed bicycle has about one of inch of rubber on the pavement at any given time. With only one set of brakes the stopping ability of this mode of transportation is minimal at best.

But being the resourceful person I am, maybe putting my feet down gently would help. For about two miles I burned the rubber off my running shoes, as well as the only working set of brake pads. I had slowed to almost thirty miles an hour by the time I got to the corner. A couple of travelers watched my plight, or should I say "flight," and when I finally got to a stop, one of the gentlemen came over to me to make sure I was okay. He said, "There was nothing to do but stand by helplessly and pray you made it without crashing." That was a profound statement, especially to this shaking, quivering mass of human flesh. I told him I needed a minute. I'm sure that equally profound statement almost brought him to gales of laughter. However, he did keep a straight face and stuck around to help me fix the bike. We replaced the front brakes I had burned up. The culprit was a wire that had come undone on the rear brakes. Consequently there was nothing to guide the brake pads onto the rubber of the tire. It all ended well, though, and that was the main thing. We need to be able to laugh at ourselves.

We then arrived at the Ice Fields which are aptly named, for the drop in temperature had us immediately donning some warmer clothing. Several Japanese tourists stopped us to ask for our pictures. We graciously supplied them with big grins and a display of fine feminine muscle. We were definitely "buff" with the several months of training for our trip, plus the rigors of the mountain terrain we had already covered. It was a challenge for us to see how long we could stay on our bikes going up these tremendous hills. I'm proud to say we achieved most without resorting to walking, and I discovered the feel of getting your second wind.

We were lean and in fine physical condition prior to

making our journey, and even more awesome when we finished. Somewhere in Japan there is a small gallery full of photos of Canadian people doing strange things. We are likely in that gallery, maybe amongst the heroes, who knows? Probably this would be wishful thinking on our part.

We met interesting people at the various campsites and tourist stops we came across. It was a trip to remember. We accomplished our trip from Jasper to Banff in three days of actual cycling although my trip was cut short by about twenty miles. When we were almost at Banff, Mark found us on a lonely stretch of highway and delivered bad news.

My Grandmother Glendora had passed away, and I needed to go home for her funeral. My friend went on to Banff alone to spend some time while I was driven to the family farm to grieve for my precious grandmother. She was the second death in my family that was so dear and close to me. I had lost my Grandpa James two years before. One of my aunts had cancer and passed away when I was young, but I hardly remember her as she lived a distance away in another province.

When my grandmother passed away, it was a time when

Mark and I were going through a rough patch in our marriage. I commend him for seeing me through my grief even though our marriage was destined not to survive.

We spent a few days with my family and then returned to Banff. We picked up my friend, and Mark drove us to Salmon Arm, British Columbia. Never being a quitter, I had decided to cycle to Kelowna, some seventy miles or so, with my friend. It was a challenging ride, not so much because I had just lost my grandmother, and she would have wanted me to finish what I started, but also because there were no shoulders at the edge of the highway.

We were exposed to traffic that was traveling fifty miles an hour (eighty kilometers per hour for those who don't do miles) with little or nowhere to move out of the way. The worst moments were when big rigs passed us as the draft pulled us toward the truck. But most people watched out for us and gave as much room as they could. We had rear view mirrors and could see approaching vehicles so were prepared when they did come upon us.

This leg of our journey gave me time to reflect and

grieve for my grannie. I spent a good deal of time in the presence of my grandmother while growing up, and she taught me much. I knew I would miss her, which I still do today. I have taped conversations with my grandmother which I cherish. I can listen to her voice when she comes to mind. If you have the opportunity to video or tape your parents and grandparents, it is a great idea. You can keep them with you in voice as well as in memory. My grannie had a distinct giggle, and whenever I miss her, I can pop in that cd and listen to her again.

Even though I was grieving at the end, our trip was a time that will forever live in our memories. Dot has forgiven me even though I did convince her to look for bear mace. We had many special moments and we kept in touch with a Christmas card each year for some time. She is still a Vancouverite at heart, loves the corporate world, and was happy to raise her children there. She has a fine man and is content in her life.

I continued to cycle to the pool every day in the summer and swim laps prior to work. In the winter I still swam and skied at least three days per week. It was good to be physically fit.

My never-ending love of horses... I have always loved time with my horses, whether it was just around the farms where I lived, out on trails, in the back country, or on mountainous terrain. Horses are special animals. They are intelligent and graceful although the odd time I've come across one who was clumsy.

I enjoyed training the young horses. There is something so special about a baby horse. I loved watching the foals learning trust first of all, and their inquisitiveness and eagerness to please always made working with them a pleasure. There were a few stubborn ones who took a little longer to train, but they were often the most loyal in the end. Each one has a different personality although there are traits passed from the stallion and mare that tend to mold them into who they are.

Patience while working with young horses can be challenging. Some horses are quite fearful and want to leave, particularly if they were not handled as babies. Sometimes it can take days for a young horse to trust you and realize he or she is not in danger. It is very rewarding when you see the change happen and the horse turns to look at you, finally allowing you to approach, and put your hand on its neck.

Once you bond with a horse, that connection is a learning curve for both of you. Knowing when that animal is frightened, frustrated, uncomfortable, or just plain confused is necessary. Repetition is also necessary. Doing something once does not usually stay with a horse.

Some of my very best memories were created while I was on the back of horses, and I can still ride for short periods. I am not training foals these days nor do I take a chance riding the young ones now. I have experienced enough buck offs and disasters that I don't want to go there anymore. I can't bounce and roll like I used to. When the horses had lots of go with maybe the odd crow hop or a tiny buck, it used to be fun. I also enjoyed standing on the back of a horse or running flat out racing with a friend or sibling. Now, slow is good, so I don't get into trouble, and most of my friends don't ride anymore for the same reason. They just plain don't want to fall off and get hurt.

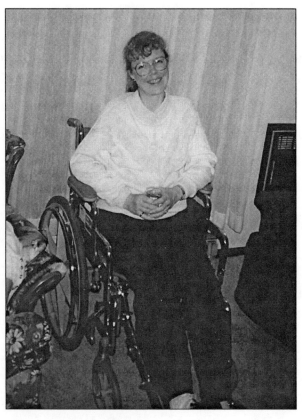

After a spinal fracture while breaking a young horse — I had another knee surgery prior to the discovery of the fracture, thus the wheelchair

My careers – nursing...I became a nursing aide in 1970, planning to work two or three years and then continue my education in the field of nursing. During our Nurse's Aide training there were three of us who did not wish to stay in residence. We knew living together in an apartment and sharing the cost of rent would save us money. We also had boyfriends and did not want structure such as the dorm provided.

None of us had wealthy parents who were paying our way, so we had little in the way of furniture. We took turns sleeping in our one single bed, which was a little softer than the floor. There was a blow up chair, lawn lounge chair, and a TV table, which doubled as our kitchen table. Somehow we made do and had a great time. Our folks did send us a little cash when they could, and we also had some funding from an unemployment insurance plan through the government. We had a resident white Persian cat named Casper. He was great company, but when the landlady discovered him, we had to become creative about his whereabouts so we wouldn't be asked to leave. Later I took Casper home for my mom to adopt, and she loved him too.

During our training I remember being left alone on

the ward one night with one other nurse while everyone else went for their break. I believe we were short staffed that particular night. We had a patient on our ward suffering from the DT's. He was in alcohol withdrawal, and many such patients experience hallucinations as they go through the detoxification process. He was in a bad way, and we were keeping a close eye on him. He had a stomach tube, catheter and intravenous line. He was confined to his bed for obvious reasons. While the other staff members were away, he suddenly came "alive" and proceeded to get out of his bed. He was throwing things around his room. The bed pan hit the wall and he was yelling. Of course he vented his frustrations on the first person he saw, yours truly.

I tried to calm him down but it was obvious he was totally out of control. He then pulled all of his tubes out so there was blood everywhere. We called for an orderly who came from another ward, and with several other nurses we were finally able to subdue him. Needless to say I was a little shaken, as his room looked like a crime scene. At this point I was certainly doubting my choice of a nursing career.

A portion of my training on the maternity ward and

nursery more than made up for that incident. I thoroughly loved the nursery but was not successful in obtaining a job there after I graduated. Only the seasoned nurses were privileged to work on those wards.

There was another situation I remember clearly. We were told by experienced nurses who had been in the profession for a time, "When there is a full moon, expect the craziness to begin." There were babies born in multitudes and anyone suffering a mental imbalance could often be tipped over the edge on those nights. A perfect example of that occurred one full moon night. There was a woman who was an amputee. I do not recall the circumstances of her amputation, but she became one of those who turned into a crazy person. It took five of us to restrain her so she would not jump out of her window which was on the fourth floor. In those days hospitals had windows which would open.

Pediatrics was a great place for me to work excepting for the little ones suffering from terminal or serious diseases. I remember a beautiful baby boy only nine months old. His parents came to see him less and less as his illness progressed. He had leukemia and was just biding his time. The doctors had given him only three months to live. The parents either did not care enough or more than likely could not bear to watch him die. We would just hold him whenever we had a break. He did not die while I was training but likely passed away shortly afterward. My nursing career almost ended during that part of my training. It bothered me a great deal to see those tiny bodies suffering so.

When my training was done there was a surplus of nurses and it was difficult to obtain work. Unfortunately we are faced with the exact opposite in nursing today. There are not enough medical staff anywhere to cover the need. At any rate I ended up taking a position on an experimental palliative care ward in a teaching hospital.

I was in no way prepared for this palliative care experience. I remember a gentleman in my care for about three months while he deteriorated from a vital person to just a shell of a man. He did not recognize some of his family during this terminal illness. He had a brain tumour which could not be surgically treated. Today he probably could have survived or had a very good chance of having his cancer in remission. He was a wonderful person and very like my own grandfather. It was difficult to watch him waste away. His cancer was aggressive and he lost his sight. It was very difficult for him to speak after a short time which made communication with his family almost impossible, so I often spoke for him as no one else could understand what he was trying to say.

I won't ever forget the day I arrived for my shift to find he had died. It was like losing a good friend.

Recently I attended the funeral of a family friend. I recognized a nurse from our local hospital and went to speak with her. When I asked if she had known my friend long; she said no, but he was often her patient. She felt a need to say good bye.

At that moment I thought maybe having done the same with my patient who had lost his battle with cancer may have helped me accept his passing more easily. Some people would say this is too much involvement with a patient, but people deal with grief in different ways, and sometimes attending the celebration of life is a successful way to gain closure.

I did leave nursing shortly after my cancer patient's death due to stress. Looking back it was likely my marriage more than anything that was causing me difficulty.

Nursing would have been a good profession for me. I believe dealing with the emotional side of losing my patients may have been easier after a time.

My next career was in the retail business...
After leaving nursing, I worked in a retail outlet shoe store. There was a young woman working there from a minority group. I befriended her for a number of reasons. Some staff were shunning her, and I felt a little sorry for her. She was suddenly fired for stealing shoes. I was so shocked and annoyed with her dishonesty. I am honest to a fault if that is possible.

While working at this same store I found fifty-two dollars while straightening a display. There was a two dollar bill in amongst some shoes and I then discovered a fifty dollar bill lying on the floor. Now bear in mind fifty dollars was a lot of money in those days, particularly for a young person with limited funds.

Being the person I am, though, reporting my find to management was the only thing to do. Ninety days later

I was called to the office and rewarded for my honesty with fifty-two dollars, as no one ever claimed it. That money made a big difference in paying my bills that month.

My parents taught us that honesty is always best even if it gets you into trouble. I always told the children in my life that honesty was best. "You may receive some punishment for the deed you did but nothing compared to what could happen by being untruthful." If more parents made that clear to their children our world might be a little better place.

After moving to another town when my husband Mark was transferred with his job, I became involved in door to door sales with a cosmetic company. I began to worry about dogs and being out after dark in areas where no one really should be walking the streets alone, so I quit.

I worked then as a store security person until I caught a young fellow stealing. He was carrying a switchblade. I sat alone with him until the police arrived. During their search of him they found the knife. I felt very uncomfortable at the possibility of violence - and here I was working for minimum wages. Not a good idea! Another good reason for leaving this job was being the last person to leave the business. I had to lock up and then walk *in the dark* to my vehicle which was some distance away.

We used to scare each other when we were children, and perhaps that is where I gained such a healthy fear of the dark. One of my chores then was to shut the chickens in at night and most times that was after the sun went down. I remember running for all I was worth to the chicken coop and back. I probably set some speed records. One time Dad had a field cultivator hooked to the tractor which was parked beside our fuel tanks. I had to pass the tractor on my way to the chicken barn. Although it was dark, I could see the tractor's outline above the barn. I made a wide enough path, I thought, to go around the tractor and avoid colliding with it. Bear in mind I was running full tilt and I crashed into that darn cultivator. To this day I have a dent in my right leg.

Anyway I digress.

After moving to Victoria, I worked in retail once again and then left their employment as company management refused to consider me for a promotion. Mark worked for an opposing store chain.

I was about to embark upon a life-changing career that would last twenty-three years. I had decided to find a job and walked up one side of Douglas Street and down the other. I would stop in front of a business and ask myself, "What could I do here?"

During my walk, I arrived at the door of an auto insurance company. It was a relatively new company then, an insurance monopoly, quite a political football really. I recalled the short time I had spent in an insurance office shortly after Mark and I married. I had enjoyed my time there, so this company seemed a good choice.

When I inquired about employment, I was advised to attend the unemployment center to see if there were any job openings, as any positions available would be posted there. Then I asked to see the manager. The manager was an affable character, and we liked each other right off. I told him I could be of assistance to this company "for sure." He asked me to fill out an application as there would be a need for some part-time help over the summer months, and he liked my gumption.

Two days later I started with the insurance company as a file clerk and worked my way up. I eventually became a claims unit manager at one of the largest offices in the province. I worked for twenty-three years with this auto insurance group, which was one of the largest in North America.

During the first year of employment shortly after a strike, as we had become a union shop, I had an opportunity to apply for a job in the Okanagan working as a claims adjuster. By this time, I had found my niche and wanted a career in insurance. As I mentioned before, Mark really wanted to move back to his home town and pursue a career as an electrician, so the timing was perfect.

The path of my insurance career... Auto insurance claims was an exciting business. I was working as a claims adjuster settling claims. I graduated from minor collisions and comprehensive type claims to bodily injury and more serious accident claims later in my career. I began managing people and running a claims office after some years in the business.

I loved the investigation and also dealing with people.

I made it my mission to settle claims fairly and treat people with the respect due them.

There were of course fraudulent claims and the seedier side of the population that we did have to deal with too. I found those challenging in many respects. It was rewarding, particularly when I was able to prove the claim was misrepresented. I had a hard time understanding why people were dishonest as I have never believed in financial gain at someone else's expense.

This career was a good fit as I was always intrigued by vehicles, and I found investigating claims interesting and challenging. I love to drive myself, and have logged many miles, not only doing the driving, but as a passenger as well. Staying out of harm's way can be a challenge sometimes, and I have avoided many situations that may have resulted in my being hurt or in hurting someone else, including the odd wild animal. I have never struck a wild animal. I know so many people that trust they will stay off the road only to find out they don't. Being aware and perhaps slowing to avoid that animal darting into your path is a really smart thing to do.

As I grew as an investigator and as a person, I had many challenges and rewards in my chosen field and met some memorable characters, both colleagues and claimants. There are a couple of claimants that immediately come to mind.

One memorable character showed up for a claim with several criminal charges as a result of his accident. We did recorded statements then, but this was one of those times where I quickly realized my claimant was "half a bubble off plum," so I turned off the recorder. His charges included evading police, speeding, dangerous driving, and avoiding arrest. Once we got into his story, I had a hard time not laughing out loud. I had to remain professional, though, for it was indeed a serious matter.

This man was actually schizophrenic, and he believed God was directing him to run from the police. He was, in fact, driving at incredibly excessive speeds through downtown streets, and the police managed to get him to a back road, where he failed to negotiate a corner and ended up going through a wooden rail fence into a strawberry field. How the pole that came through the motor and into the passenger compartment missed him is indeed a miracle, so maybe God was part of that scenario. The driver, however, was able to get out of his vehicle and sprint across the strawberry field with police officers in hot pursuit. All the while he was yelling back at the officers to get the other guy! Anyway, we finally managed to get his claim resolved, and he was not allowed to drive anymore. It was quite a funny scenario but sad at the same time.

Another situation I remember was when two young guys arrived at the claims office in a brand new Marquis, a beautiful car that was beautiful no more. It was drivable, but they had to crawl through the windows to get in and out of the vehicle. The hood was also tied down with a wire to prevent it from flying up into the windshield. Both ends of the vehicle were curled upward. The vehicle was actually owned by the driver's dad. The driver was sixteen years old and had only recently achieved the wonderful privilege of getting his driver's license. He begged his dad to let him drive the new car, just take it for a little spin. Dad relented and the little spin ended up in Spokane, Washington. The friend had generously agreed to come along for the ride.

Well, as fate would have it the boys ended up on a one-way street going the wrong way. They saw an out and took it. There was a cement pad to the right that looked like it was an entrance to a parking lot. It was. However, they had to go down a flight of cement steps to get into said parking lot. Luckily no one was injured, except for the automobile of course.

As I mentioned, the car was at a distinct angle on both ends, and how they ever drove the thing, let alone got back across the border without being stopped by police, I shall never know. They weren't willing to share those little details.

So when you smash up Dad's brand new car, you apparently do not go home, but to Grandma's house, a few hundred miles from home. She sent the boys straight to us. Despite their pleas, I did have to call Dad and tell him where the car was and ask him questions about its use, how the boys came to be in it and in a different country when the damage occurred.

Needless to say Dad was livid and started screaming at me. I calmed him down long enough to have him talk, or should I say, scream at his son. We then had to call the police in Washington to make sure no one was injured and no other vehicles were involved. The officer knew about said incident and they were looking for the vehicle, so he promptly started yelling – at me. I explained for the second time who I was, not the driver of this vehicle, but that I had the young fellow in front of me. The officer could certainly speak with him I said.

We eventually got it sorted out. The car was repaired before Dad saw it, and he promptly sold the car. The son stayed at his Grandma's for the duration of the school year. He knew it was safer as I'm sure his Dad was mad at him for the whole time.

But, can you imagine the Starsky and Hutch scenario that unfolded in the parking lot that day? Oh my gosh! It would have been pretty funny to see the look of horror on those kids' faces as they bounced down the cement stairs to that parking lot.

There were many more stories and many more interesting claims, but I think the claims that were most interesting were bodily injury ones, not from a morbid point of view but from the investigative side of claims adjusting. I enjoyed working with the police officers, claimants and their families, and other professionals that I came in contact with. Lawyers, doctors, and other health practitioners were involved in the resolution of injury claims. Plus there were often liability issues to be hashed out with claims people from other companies, different provinces, and even other countries.

I learned so much and with my nursing background, understanding bodily injury and the recovery process came easily. I also discovered a great deal about the trajectory of bodies and items within the vehicle during a crash, and the usage of seatbelts. When I began my career, there was still much controversy over the use of seatbelts. Trust me, with the research and statistics that have been compiled, you are inarguably better off wearing a seatbelt. The chances of you dying with the belt on are FAR less than without it!

I became involved in groups, committees, and community events on behalf of the insurance company. I spoke at schools regarding seatbelt usage, drinking, drugs, speeding, and a number of other vehicle related issues.

There were classes for drivers convicted of alcohol related offenses. I felt there might have been a few of those people that were actually impacted by my presentations, but most *had* to be there so their hearts weren't in it – unfortunately.

I was part of the group that designed and promoted school crosswalk wooden cut-outs of children for school zones. The fact I am one of the people responsible for those signs is gratifying. I may have helped save some child from injury or death.

I was a lead player on a committee organized to solve hit and run accidents. We partnered with police, auto body repair shops, and claims staff. We solved many claims where both parties involved in a collision claimed hit and run. We matched up the vehicles with help from all three committee members by comparing our lists and calling the vehicle owners to report for match up sessions. In the end it just wasn't productive time for the amount of money we saved policy holders. We abandoned part of the program but maintained parking lot signs encouraging witnesses to report hit and run accidents to police or claims staff.

There was another task force in which I played a major role. It was an innovative hands-on team of adjusters. When a serious motor vehicle accident occurred, the police would call us to the scene. We had a claims adjuster on call twenty-four hours per day. There was a list of vehicle rental companies, hotels which could provide rooms quickly, a trauma counsellor, and other specialists and service providers available at short notice. This made the process much easier for those involved in serious accidents. It was a first for the company, and our policy holders were very receptive to this concept. We helped many folk, especially claimants from out of town. We also saved the company money when claimants did not run to a lawyer after they saw how fairly we treated them. Insurance company management did not feel it was financially beneficial to pay for overtime on call-outs for my staff, so we had to abandon the program. I still believe it was not only helpful to our policy holders but also cost effective in the long run and great public relations.

I judged high school speech competitions which was fun. I also did interviews with newspaper and television staff concerning the various projects I was involved in. I was the "Smile of the Week" for the local paper one time, nothing to do with the company, but fun anyway. I don't recall just how that person was chosen as the "Smile of the Week," but my picture was in the paper. I do have a sunny outlook on life and I am always smiling.

It was an honor to be chosen, along with eleven other staff members from throughout the province, as committee members plotting the future for our company in many important areas. We were sequestered in a conference room for an entire week. Armed with a number of surveys and flip charts, our committee brainstormed. There were no suggestions that went unheeded by our group. The result was a three hundred page document which we presented to the company's board. Most of our suggestions have been implemented over the last several years. I was pleased to be one of the chosen few for this project.

Many times after hours my staff unit could be found working alongside me without pay, particularly if we had a project to complete. I never asked more of my staff than I was prepared to do myself.

I was perhaps a manager a little ahead of my time when it came to working projects and thinking outside of the box. I once took my claims unit away from the office into another staff member's back yard. My team booked themselves out so there were no calls or appointments, and we brainstormed for two hours beside this lady's pool, put a plan together, and completed it three months ahead of schedule. I was highly criticized for taking my gang away from the office, but that two hours was the most productive time we had ever spent together. Our project was highly successful. When your staff buy into an idea, you can bet it will come to fruition.

I managed a small claims office on my own for a few years. It was challenging as several of the staff were either my peers or older than myself. Being a woman in a position of authority with a company that was still basically male oriented had many moments of difficulty as well.

I recall a conversation with my supervisor before becoming a manager myself. I was not one to wear much makeup and did not wear suits often. He was quite blunt about image playing a huge role for me in gaining the respect of my staff. He said, "Not only will you be managing men, but men who are older than yourself and other employees who are and have been your peers for some time. There will be judgement, jealousy, and insubordination to deal with. You need to look like the professional manager I know you can be." He suggested I start wearing makeup and suits. At first I was a bit offended but quickly realized he was absolutely right!

After a few years I moved back to the bigger office as a unit manager. I supervised one of the largest units of claims staff in the company. I became a victim of corporate indifference a few years later when my manager took on some staff as his responsibility. I could not keep up with the workload simply because of volume. We were an extremely busy office with huge volumes of serious accident claims.

To be fair my manager had more than he could handle as well. He was trying to help us through a tough time when we did not have enough staff. He could not justify hiring another middle manager as our budget certainly wouldn't allow for one.

As fate would have it, an examiner from another office, a fellow who was looking to make a name for himself, found settlements he felt were unwarranted during some file reviews. The staff in question were those two gentlemen whom my manager was going to assist, but on paper they were still my employees. The files examined showed settlements over the monetary authority of these two adjusters. The files had no "red ink," or in other words there was no management guidance before settlement of the claims.

Consequently there was an investigation that lasted over a month, with all of these adjusters' files being examined in minute detail. We became three under the microscope, and my computer was frozen shortly after the investigation began. I was wise enough to print copies of important information before the investigators took that step.

Thankfully I had documented conversations and agreements between my manager and myself regarding his involvement. He had those two adjusters reporting directly to him, but because of his own workload, there had been no time to assist them. The adjusters were more or less flying on their own. The settlements they made were within reason, but the red ink was not there to support their decisions. I believed in offering fair settlements with proper documentation, but there was still a point where the adjuster needed guidance.

This experience was devastating, not only for the two employees involved, but for myself and a number of my other staff as well. The two adjusters were both responsible fellows, and I was a dedicated employee with twenty-three years of service. I was good at my job so to go through an investigation implicating my staff members and myself with being anything but forthright was unjustified, hurtful to us all, and handled very poorly.

I was presented with ridiculous options which upper

management truly hoped would be acceptable to me. The offers included a decrease in pay scale, a lesser position, a move to a large city and an office where the cost of living far exceeded what I currently was experiencing. They thought I would resign, but my reputation, honesty and everything I had worked for all those years was at stake.

Fortunately my fall from grace was not justified by the company, and a labour lawyer assisted me in obtaining a fair settlement in the end.

My manager retired from the company shortly after, also with a settlement.

This experience left me with a bitter taste in my mouth for a very long time. I had given my heart and soul to this company, and being treated in this manner was difficult at best. My self-esteem took a real kick and I swore I would never work for a corporate employer again. You truly are just a number in most corporations.

In the end I told myself, "Don't look back, you're not going that way." It did take quite a while for me to forgive those that put me in the position of having to defend my reputation and honesty.

I realized recently that I had truly forgiven my manager for his part in this whole scenario. He did not defend me or accept responsibility for what happened. At least I was given the impression he did not. I saw him in a parking area just months ago and said hello to him. He did not know who it was, but he wanted a hug when I told him my name. I hugged him back and asked him how he was doing. He did want to know about my life too and I felt the forgiveness was already there. I hope his life is good.

I still miss investigation, and working with claimants but am glad to be away from the corporate nightmare. I hit the glass ceiling several times during my career with this company but managed to move forward and upward anyway. There still exists some barriers for women, even now, some sixteen years since I left the insurance company. Although there are many more women in those higher profile management positions, their pay scales often do not reflect that.

Saving my mortal soul... My marriage had dissolved early in my insurance career, and for a while I simply "went off the rails." There were too many men, too much alcohol and partying, all of which was hard on my reputation, psyche, and body. There was more than once that I dragged myself into work with little or no sleep and was still very likely impaired. I'm not sure what I was looking for but I certainly didn't find it living that kind of lifestyle.

I could go into a great lot of detail here, but in the interest of protecting my innocent grandchildren, I will not expound on my escapades, except to say they were some pretty wild times, and I don't recommend any one of them go down that road.

I will give you one little example of foolishness which I'm sure stopped a few hearts while in progress. Once at a pub, and after several drinks when I was feeling quite immortal, I proceeded to walk on a hand rail some twenty feet above the floor just to prove I could. We did lots of tightrope walking when we were kids, and I was sure it was still easy for me to do. Despite my inebriated state, it was a success, but had I slipped, the results could have been catastrophic.

Thanks to a few good friends and some old fashioned values, I eventually dragged myself away from the downward spiral I was on. Life wasn't really enjoyable for me, and finding whatever I was looking for wasn't happening.

During all of this turmoil, I met Bob, a traffic analyst with the police department. It was all very innocent in the beginning. We became good friends while working on a number of case files together. It was a great way to start a relationship. One day, Bob asked if it would be alright to bring his little girls to the acreage where I kept my mare so they could have horseback rides.

I fell in love with those kids the first day. Within a few months, Bob's marriage dissolved, and he moved out on his own. We started looking at our relationship in a different way, and it surprised me how much feeling I had developed for this man. I would later become step-mother to his girls, although if anyone had said that, I wouldn't have believed them.

I understood Bob's occupation and passion for discovering details of an accident. I was involved in the same investigative field on a smaller scale and relied on his expertise many times when determining liability. We investigated many incidents together, and I learned so much from him. I highly respected his knowledge and ability, and we travelled to seminars to learn even more.

I was forced to take vacation time for attending these seminars. I was not reimbursed for any expenses, but my manager expected me to share my knowledge upon returning to my job. That was quite unfair, but I was intrigued with investigation and willing to share. Besides, crashing cars was so much fun!

After retiring from the police force, Bob joined his friend's private accident re-construction business. Bob and his friend organized an association for technical accident investigators which included engineers, police-men, and private investigators from across the country. I was fortunate to become an associate member of that organization. Each year there was a seminar in Canada or the United States which we usually attended.

At these seminars I watched driver's crash vehicles and slide them on wet and dry surfaces to witness what happened during a crash. We calculated stopping and sliding distances, and I learned how to determine seat-belt usage and bodily impact. At one seminar we had a pedestrian crash dummy. It was interesting to see what his body did during different scenarios. The guys gave the test dummy a bag of groceries, sunglasses, a hat and shoes, and stood him up. They then had a truck hit him at different speeds to determine how it affected the movement of his body. We were able to appreciate distances and the force of impact. I can tell you groceries covered an area of over three hundred feet at a speed of forty kilometers per hour. The hat and running shoes stayed right where he was standing when the vehicle hit him. His body flew right out of those articles and through the air until contacting the vehicle or pavement.

He was then put on a bicycle and the truck hit him again. The bicycle wheel stuck into the front of the pickup truck. Mr. Pedestrian sailed over the cab after impacting the windshield. I'm pretty sure we killed him that time.

It was very interesting to see what actually took place in a pedestrian knockdown even though it was in a controlled environment. Bob and I came across a pedestrian accident for real once. Because of my medical background and the knowledge we both had acquired in investigation, along with Bob's police experience, we were able to be of great assistance at that accident scene.

We attended a seminar in Boise, Idaho, and did some touring there, including the facility where we saw the first heart transplant recipient, a cow. Visiting Salt Lake City up close on another seminar trip was a great learning experience too!

I handled a pedestrian fatality claim which Bob was investigating. With the help of some private accident investigators, we re-enacted this tragedy. I played the role of victim. We used the striking vehicle and witnesses with their vehicles to assist us with the re-enactment. There was an accident investigator and a film man in the striking vehicle. They timed the lighting so the conditions mirrored the actual event. We had decreased the speed of all vehicles to ensure safety. I was to walk across the road to the centre line and stop. I had to cross between the two oncoming witness vehicles. The striking vehicle was then to go around me as cameras were rolling. I could tell the driver did not see me as the car approached. I was wearing dark clothing similar to what the deceased pedestrian had been wearing. Needless to say I did not stop at the centre line, but got the heck out of his way. I did not play the role of victim in any more re-enactments let me tell you. We did learn a great deal, however, about what took place the night of that particular incident by pushing replay.

My father was impressed with Bob at once. After all he knew how to harness a team of horses. The first day they met Bob and I arrived at a hunting camp where my dad was guiding some German hunters. Dad needed a team of horses harnessed, so Bob got right to it. He's told me since the harness was a set he had never handled before. He was learning as the harness went on.

Bob is a good old farm boy from Saskatchewan, so he understood my father. Today Dad considers Bob one of his boys, and this Saskatchewan farm boy certainly looks at Dad as a father too. We have been very fortunate to have had two very special dads: his and mine. They are totally different but equally special. I went on to marry Bob, the farmer/policeman many years later.

I thank God for bringing him into my life when he did.

On our wedding day with my life partner Bob

Dealing with criminals... My first experience with a criminal happened while Mark and I lived in Calgary Alberta. There was a man who came to the store where Mark worked. He regularly had coffee with and befriended my ex-husband and several other people in the area. The man claimed he worked for a large insurance company and flashed his money around all of the time, leading people to believe he had a great deal of it. One day he asked Mark to loan him five hundred dollars until Friday as he wanted to buy his wife a fur coat for her birthday. He claimed to have a big check coming in right away. He said he would put his car up as collateral and signed a piece of paper to that effect.

Mark did have the foresight to check the serial number on the vehicle. No money showed up, and when Mark and I went to collect the loan, the man was not home. His wife had just discovered her husband's deceit and the fact he was a fraud. She had been drinking, and when he arrived, she confronted him about his dishonesty. That was my first real experience with domestic violence. He hit her and said, "Go to the bedroom. You are embarrassing me!"

I followed her and we talked. She was understandably very distraught. She started to sound a little strange and wasn't making any sense. I did get her to tell me she had taken some pills as well as the alcohol. Thank goodness for my nurses training. I called Mark and said we must get her to the hospital immediately as she was in trouble.

While Mark and the lady's husband were getting her to the car, she passed out. I told them to put her in the back seat with me and drive. We were only a few short blocks from the hospital, and enroute I lost her pulse. I started CPR immediately and regained a pulse, although it was thready, by the time we got to the hospital. I gave the required information to the doctor and then proceeded to have a meltdown. I cried for this girl, not only for what she was experiencing, but for what she may have endured at the hands of her husband.

My patient did recover and went on to divorce her husband, and he spent some time in jail. He had duped many people including a police office and several other businessmen. Because we had the correct serial number and a signed bill of sale, we ended up with the car. It was a beautiful car, a top of the line Riviera, but it quit running while we were on our way to a friends' home for Christmas. There was a terrible storm that night, and we weren't prepared for a vehicle breakdown. If anyone tells you there is no Santa Claus, do not believe them. We met him that night. A man stopped and helped us get that car mobile enough to drive. When we turned to say thank you, he was gone. Don't ask me where he went. To this day I do not know.

My next experience with the less desirable side of society was the incident I previously described when I was employed as a store detective.

Sometime in the early eighties when my marriage had taken a turn for the worse I was living alone. My house was in a quiet neighborhood. We neighbors all knew one another and often during hot summer nights and into the fall, we left our doors open so cool night air could come into the house. Summer temperatures often reached ninety to one hundred degrees Fahrenheit. The screen doors kept any unwanted crawly creatures out. We never worried about strangers.

That changed one particular night near the end of summer. It had cooled off considerably that night so I started a wood fire. I had a beautiful central fireplace. The fire had burned down, and as I opened the back door to get more wood, I saw a strange man in the backyard. I immediately went on the offense which he was not expecting, guaranteed. I started berating him loudly. He turned tail and ran with me in hot pursuit. WHAT A FOOLISH THING TO DO!!! It was dark and I chased that guy halfway down the street. I'm pretty sure he was a Peeping Tom, otherwise the out-come may have been quite different. Once I realized

I might be in trouble if he stopped, I quit chasing him and went back to my house.

Some years later when Bob and I were living together there was another experience with the unsavory element. My property backed onto a main roadway so I could see into my backyard driving home from work. On the day in question I noticed a man at my kitchen window. Did I stop at the neighbors and call Bob or the police? NO… I proceeded to whip into the driveway, with flourish I might add, and jumped from my truck. I left the truck running with the door open. I ran around the back of the house and stopped the guy short with a gruff, "What are you doing here?" He was in the process of vaulting over a brick wall between the patio and my back yard. It was summer and really very light out. The young man was tall and carried a duffle bag. He was quite startled by my bravery and said, "I was just passing through". I told him, "No you weren't, you were at my kitchen window, and I want to know just what you were doing." Now, bear in mind Bob was a member of the police force and was usually home prior to me. Normally there would have been a police car in the driveway that time of day.

I approached this guy just like a little "banty" rooster, upset that he would be looking into my house ("banty" roosters are little but have the heart of a lion. They just think they are big!) When the intruder saw he was not going to convince me he was "just passing through," he decided to run. Here I was again, chasing a man through the neighborhood. This time I was in a suit with high heels and a tight skirt. It must have been quite a sight. I don't know that anyone saw it though. I gave up the chase after crossing the yards of three neighbours. The would-be thief was tall and had a distinct advantage with longer legs and no high heels. I truly do not know what would have happened had I caught him. He was certainly far bigger than me. After I gave up the chase, I went back to my house, shut off my truck, and went inside… to make sure there was no one else around. What was I thinking? I was just annoyed that this guy had the audacity to be on my property without an invitation.

Thank goodness there was no one else in my house. As I waited for Bob to arrive, there was a swishing sound in the kitchen. I discovered the screen of my kitchen window had been cut on three sides. It took a very sharp object to do that.

I didn't wait any longer for Bob to arrive. I called the police station and reported the event. While waiting for the police, I went to the backyard again and discovered a perfect footprint on a wooden jockey box Bob had built. We had just painted it the day before, and the paint was fresh. The bad guy was apprehended just a few weeks later, and the footprint the police were able to lift from that jockey box helped to identify him. He admitted to fifty-three break and enters in the area. I still get a little queasy thinking about what could have happened just a few minutes later had I caught him in my house. Needless to say, I received a lecture from Bob. "Never confront anyone like that again. Go to the neighbours and call the police," he ordered sternly.

Probably the only reason the thief ran was a confrontation was not what he expected. I don't recommend confronting a criminal. In the first situation I should have shut the door, locked it, and called the authorities. In the second incident I ought to have gone to the neighbors and called the police, which would have been a far better choice. Chances are pretty good the guy would have been nabbed that day instead of two weeks later.

Dads...I had very strong male role models during my growing up years and am maybe a little too brave as a result. Two of those role models I was privileged to call "Dad."

My father-in-law, Dad H, was a farmer in Saskatchewan and did not expect any more from life than a living and the successful upbringing of his two boys. He was a devoted husband, although demanding, and was very proud that both sons became members of the Royal Canadian Mounted Police. Dad H was cynical, judgmental, and quick to comment on what others were doing. He gave names to those people walking outside his home. For example, the man who picked up trash as he was walking was "Mr. Pickup."

My father-in-law loved me like most dads love their daughters. He didn't have any girls and I felt cherished and special when I was with him. He and I spent many hours together at our acreage working with the animals, picking fruit, mending fences, and just hanging out together. We even buried our old dog one day and shared a moment of grief.

Once Dad H and I were picking apples at our acreage. The tree was very tall. I was standing on the top of a twelve foot ladder and reaching farther. Dad H was quite worried so I convinced him to put a ladder in the bucket of the tractor, and to my surprise, he helped me do that. Having the ladder there was likely more precarious than my standing on the top of the ladder.

Dad H accompanied my husband and me once on a horse back trip with our daughters and my family. He surely showed his mettle on that excursion. It was also the first and last time I ever saw my father-in-law take a drink of alcohol.

Dad H enjoyed many horseback rides with us, whether it was just around the acreage and orchards, up into the hills or away. We spent hours with the horses just at our acreage. Dad H liked to drive horses as he spent many years on the farm working with them when there was no machinery to do the work. He later enjoyed riding horses with his sons.

Dad H was soft hearted and cared more about most things than he showed. My husband is very like him in so many ways. In later years Dad H's health deteriorated and he struggled with the debilitating disease, Alzheimer's. He spent most of his time sitting in his chair just watching people and traffic out his balcony window. It was very hard to watch this once vital man slowly succumb to this dreadful disease. Unfortunately Alzheimer's tends to run in families, so it may be something that could haunt us again a few years down the road.

We recently buried Dad H in a cemetery that borders the farm property where he grew up, farmed, and raised his own family. It is a peaceful and very beautiful place.

Dad… Remembering you is easy, I do it every day. Missing you is the heartache that never goes away.

My own father, on the other hand, is a "mountain man". Dad is a big man with huge hands, a warm heart, and a generous hug. He calls a spade a spade and doesn't take much guff from anybody. Dad loves the outdoors and rode horse back on a mountain trip for the last time when he was eighty-one. He went on pack trips with family into the mountains usually for several weeks most summers for many years. We family members have many cherished memories as a result.

Dad has been through spinal surgery twice and a fused ankle, which has resulted in struggles with walking and constant chronic pain. Dad recently had a surgery for colon cancer which he surprisingly survived at the ripe young age of eighty-five. He had reacted badly to the pain medications and anesthetic. Dad was very anxious as we all would be when the anesthetics and pain medications caused him to hallucinate. Many elderly folk experience this kind of reaction to such medications especially when they have not taken much if any medication in their past. The anti-psychotic drugs were to keep him calm. Those medications were quickly sending him over the top mentally, and he was becoming increasingly anxious.

I finally convinced his doctors to quit the anti-psychotic medications and let him go home for a day. We never returned him to the hospital: instead we got him back on the medications he was taking prior to surgery, and he hasn't looked back. Dad is extremely frustrated with his lot in life as a senior, having to depend on the use of walkers and scooters. He's stubborn and cusses in front of anybody. Nonetheless, he loves his kids and worries about all of us, giving advice we don't necessarily heed. Of course we all have his Scottish roots and the stubbornness attached to that, so we have to do things our own way.

My dad has changed a lot since we grew up. We had a healthy fear of him when we were young, which was partly due to his stature. That fear has changed to a general respect for the man he is, although I think if he got angry at one of us even today, that healthy fear would come back in a rather big hurry.

I can remember him only once taking his belt to me. My brother and I were fighting, and we both ended up getting strapped with dad's belt. He only had to speak loudly or threaten us after that. My brother and I still argue about whose fault it was.

My dad believes in God and is quietly spiritual which would definitely surprise some people. Dad and I stood on a mountain top overlooking three mountain ranges one time while on a horseback trip. He put his arm around me and said, "You can't get much closer to God than this kid." He doesn't talk about God or his religious beliefs and it surprised me. It was a very special moment for us both. Only an hour earlier he was cussing my sister and me for getting too close to the edge of a shale ridge with our horses.

As tough and strong as my dad is, he's terribly afraid of heights. Because of that phobia, I had to paint the granaries at home while he worried about me being so high on the ladder. What I didn't know until many years later is he's also afraid to fly. This only makes sense, but I had never thought about it until I took him with me to the east coast of Canada for a vacation. We were in an airplane for about six hours each way. He didn't say anything to me about being fearful, and I knew he had flown before so I didn't question him.

While we were driving along the cliffs of the Cabot Trail, he nearly had a fit. He was constantly asking me if the brakes were good on the rental car and telling me: "Slow down!" "Don't get too close to the edge!" At one point I got out to look at the view. The edge of the road dropped off probably five hundred feet or more straight down to the sea. It was beautiful. Dad wouldn't leave the car and nearly stroked out on me I'm sure. Needless to say, we didn't spend much time there. The trip was very enjoyable though, and we both had an awesome time. We met distant cousins and did sightseeing in the areas where his mother and dad had grown up. It is a time with my dad I shall never forget. We had fun together seeing and experiencing so much.

At the ripe young age of seventy-two my father rode

horseback for sixteen hours through bush country he had never traversed before and crossed rivers that were extremely high in order to help one of the men who was travelling with him. The rest of dad's group stayed with the ailing friend until he got back. Understand this was in the Wilderness Park many miles from help with no cell phones or any way to call for assistance.

Dad finally reached a place where he could have someone get help. Within two hours of reaching his destination, Dad and a helicopter were at his friend's side. Dad was able to direct the pilot and arrive at the exact location of his pack group and sick friend. Two hours later the man was in surgery for a ruptured appendix. Dad's friend thankfully survived and rode on more pack trips with my father. That frantic ride definitely took its toll on my dad's health though. He was never one hundred percent after.

At this stage in my dad's life he has said several times he does not want to live in a nursing home. He is happy with his life. He knows my brothers, sisters, and I are all in a good place. We have healthy relationships, and our children are doing well. Dad's concerns are only that his wife and all the offspring enjoy the rest of their lives. He has worried about me a great deal because of the health issues I have encountered, and there is rarely a day when we don't talk at least once, whether in person or by telephone.

My mothers...I have also experienced the love of more than one mother and had several other strong female figures in my life. The women on my mother's side of the family have shown me great strength and much wisdom. They all believe the whole family raises a child, which is evident in how we look after each other's children and grandchildren within our family circle.

I spent a lot of time with one aunt in the summers, especially when I was very young and my mother needed help looking after me. Aunty Evelyn was a special person in my life and I did look to her for guidance. I am close with all of my aunts, and we talk with some regularity. We all allow ourselves to be "busy" though and unfortunately those talks do not happen often enough.

My own mother was instrumental in not only shaping my path in life but also mentoring, encouraging me, soothing my aches and pains (mental or physical), and generally being a role model. She showed me not only strength and discipline but also care and compassion for others. Mom was always strong in the face of adversity. She was and is even to this day a very positive person. Mom has a great sense of humour, even once engaging in a butter fight while making pizza with our cousins. She dressed up for Halloween. She taught us to laugh at ourselves and literally and figuratively how to "dance in the rain."

Mom worked hard throughout her life, and she taught us to understand and develop strong work ethics, an admirable trait we brothers and sisters all have ingrained in us.

Mom was a very busy mother with six children, some of us quite close in age. One time on an excursion to town we parked and walked to the grocery store. There were four of us and we were quite young. I remember holding on to Mom's coat; Norman had a harness on him with his leash in her hand; Johnny was in the stroller she was pushing, and baby Kate was in Mom's arms. Definitely there were challenges for Mom when grocery shopping, but she had us all under control, and accomplished what we came for in record time.

She was a master at organizing her time with six children. Our house was always messy but it wasn't dirty and we had a wonderful life. Mom often played with us, she helped with us with our homework, and managed to keep six healthy, happy, inquisitive children from getting into too much trouble.

Mom loved the outdoors, gardening, her flowers, reading, and just being with her children and grandchildren. She was by our side when we were sick or needed to talk. We were scolded when there needed to be discipline, but she loved us unconditionally. My youngest brother had speed on his side one time when Mom threatened to take a whip to him. Mom never would have struck him with the whip, but she must have been pretty mad to even entertain picking it up. Johnny made it all the way across the yard, through the gate, and into the barnyard before turning around and begging Mom not to whip him. He learned his lesson and never did anything to get her that mad again. Johnny is likely the only one that remembers what he was being punished for.

There was one time I wanted to go to the Green Door, a local night club, with some new friends. Mom had heard stories about the Green Door and told me she wouldn't be letting me go there. There were rumours of drugs and alcohol being used and sold in that establishment. I was only sixteen at the time. I put up quite a fuss so she told me: "Go to your room and think about it." After a little pity party, I went back downstairs and told her, "Thanks Mom, I didn't really want to go anyway. They would just be drinking."

Mom was an active senior, spending time attending her children and grandchildren's functions, sewing, golfing, curling, playing cards, lawn bowling, camping and dancing, including square dance calling. Mom enjoyed time with her friends and she was always available if anyone needed help. She worked a few different home based businesses and was very successful with those ventures. Mom joined my Mary Kay team to supplement her income. She was still a working member of my team when her stroke ended her active lifestyle at the age of seventy-four.

My mom once told me when she turned eighty she

wanted to go downtown, sit on a curb while wearing a purple hat, and spit. My mother was permanently in a wheelchair by this time due to a disabling stroke. There is an ancient bylaw in our city that dictates no spitting on the sidewalk. Mom is just enough of a rebel so I told her we would do it. We went with several of her friends and family. We all wore red and purple hats and had a jolly time spitting sunflower seeds off the curb on Main Street. We sang happy birthday at the top of our lungs. Mom thoroughly enjoyed the day.

If it seems my mother is a saint, she definitely comes close. Mom has shown us such strength and courage, particularly in these last years. She is completely bed-ridden at this time, having been paralyzed now for over nine years, and confined to a wheelchair for eight. She did not lose her voice so has been able to talk and sing with us. There are some days when her mind gets lost due to her health and medication, but mostly we are blessed to have her beautiful spirit, her love, her voice, and her humour to surround us.

The great-grandchildren have given Mom much joy since she has been in bed. The family is good about bringing their new babies for Mom to touch and feel.

She is pretty much blind now, so baby cuddles are special.

Despite her challenges, she remains alert and maintains her sense of humour. If someone complains about the weather, she will comment; "Well, we do live in Northern Alberta you know." She can recite the books of the Bible in order even to this day. She will often make some teasing comments with her caregivers. They all love her and treat her well as a result, although I have been her advocate on occasion, making sure everything is up to standard with her care.

We are close to losing our mother now as her health has declined steadily these past few months. Mom will be missed dearly, and I look toward that day with both fear and gladness. She will no longer have to suffer, but it means the devastating loss of my dear mother.

My mothers-in-law are also wonderful women and have taught me much throughout the years. Both of these ladies are also strong women, having had to work hard through their lives, and they are very much family oriented as well.

Mother H is extremely active with church and gives

much of her time to service groups and charitable activities. She is now ninety years of age and just gave up a couple of executive positions in these organizations but only because the local chapters were disbanding and no longer active.

She continues to live independently although she is now in a senior's facility. I think Mother H is enjoying the fact she no longer has to cook, and her time is her own. With Dad H no longer with us and her sons and grandchildren grown, she can now relax, spend time playing cards, and visit with friends at the lodge. Mother H also gets out occasionally to go shopping or sight-seeing and manages to get to church nearly every Sunday.

I gave you some insight into my ex mother-in-law's wisdom and love previous to this point, but I have to say she is a very inspiring lady as well. She lost her sight in one eye not long ago and now has a glass eye. When I called to inquire after her health following surgery, her comment was, "I just don't see too good. Otherwise everything is fine." I enjoy her sense of humour and good spirit.

My role as a step-mom...I want to tell you now about my life with Bob and my stepchildren. As I previously mentioned, I could not have children of my own. Mark and I had applied to adopt a child, and few months after he left, I received a call from the agency asking to attend for a home visit. I told them, "My husband and I are no longer together. It would not be fair for a baby to have only one parent when there are so many families wanting a child. I have to work and my marriage is over." I love children and was totally heart-broken. When I graduated from high school, one of my goals was to have about a dozen children and become a nurse. The career was to come first, of course.

So when two little girls, Bob's daughters, came into my life, I felt truly blessed. I met Cassandra, who was eight, and Dawn, who was five, when their Dad brought them for a horseback ride. I fell in love with them almost immediately. They enjoyed being with us and the horses, so it may have been a little easier transition for them when I became part of their family later.

Bob and I began living together almost a year later, and had his little girls on weekends. We didn't have a television, so when Cassandra and Dawn came over, they spent many hours being creative. I remember them making a car from a big cardboard box. They even had a key cut out of cardboard. They spent hours making Barbie "stuff." It was amazing what they created with paper, scissors, tape, cardboard, crayons and paints. Cassandra and Dawn had their own little store with a cash register, and both had wallets with inventive credit cards, driver's licenses, and monopoly money. The girls had their Barbies shopping in the make-believe store. Barbies came home with tiny grocery bags full of paper groceries, including tomatoes. I think there are still some little treasures in my tote of special memories. Bob also helped the girls make Barbie waterbeds with bladders from wine boxes and wooden bed frames.

I taught them to use large juice cans for stilts. I would cut holes in the large cans and weave binder twine through them, then attach the cans to the bottom of the girls' feet. They had great fun and as a special bonus, the lawn was aeriated.

I remember encouraging their imaginations. I recalled how inventive my siblings and I were when we were children. If you give a child a box, paper and scissors, it's amazing what they can do. Many of you likely have witnessed babies with presents on their first birthdays and Christmas'. They will play with boxes and paper as much if not more than the toys.

Bob's ex-wife was very bitter over their separation and divorce, so unfortunately these two beautiful little girls ended up in the middle. Too often I see couples do this to their children. It is not the children's fault regardless of circumstance, and it garners no satisfaction for anyone. There are no good divorces and everyone loses, especially the children. One of my friend's daughters got tired of her mom saying that dad was the reason they weren't together, and it was all his fault. That little girl told her mother, "Mom, I didn't choose him, you did, and he is still my dad!" I was very proud of her putting things in perspective.

My husband's job as an accident re-constructionist had him traveling and spending time away from us often. Many times my girls and I would go riding horseback on our own or travel together without him. We had many memorable days and experiences.

I recall one horseback ride in particular. I owned a young horse at the time and was just getting to know her. She was what we call "green broke," knowing some of what you wanted her to do, but not at all certain how to react to many situations. This particular day we rode our steeds up into the hills on a dusty trail. The girls wanted to gallop their horses. I was behind them and was literally eating their dust. I told them to go ahead, and I would catch up once the dust settled. My mount became pretty agitated with being left behind so after holding her back for a time, I let her run to catch the girls. You can see this unfolding right?

We were going so fast that my little mare could not negotiate a curve on the trail and off into the bush we went still running flat out. My horse was jumping stumps and skirting trees, but we weren't slowing down a whole lot. I didn't grab for leather until one of my feet slipped out of the stirrup. Back onto the trail we came. We flew by my daughters at Mach speed. Their eyes were like saucers but mine likely were too. Some distance down the trail, I eventually got my horse under control and came back to meet them. I am sure my girls thought that was the last they would see of their step-mom, at least in one piece.

When the girls were seven and ten years old, we bought

them each a horse of their own for Christmas. The first thing Dawn's little Frosty did was buck her off. He was a Kanata pony and had been used as a chariot racer prior to our purchasing him. My husband rode him, but he obviously had never been ridden by a child, so he likely thought she was some pesky little critter. He didn't want her on his back anyway. Frosty tossed her a couple of times afterward and shook her confidence pretty badly. In hindsight he was one of those purchases we would rather not have made even if he was a cute little guy.

Cassandra had a great mare. Beauty was a wonderful kids' horse, and we had her for a number of years. Sadly we lost her when she suffered a bad bout of colic. She had been pastured with goats for some years prior to our buying her and was what we horse people call an easy keeper. We had to watch that she didn't overeat, and sometimes just a change in the weather would give her a tummy ache. She had a big hay belly, and I recall once a veterinarian insisting Beauty was pregnant even though my husband told her the mare had not been exposed to a stallion. The vet did a pregnancy check anyway, and of course, she was "open," or not in foal. My husband was so disgusted with that veterinarian he never called her again.

Later we acquired another horse, a twelve-year-old named Buck. It was an ironic name because he never did buck. His name came from his coloring which was buckskin. We purchased him from the famous Douglas Lake Ranch. He was a great fellow and gave Dawn her confidence back. She spent many fun-filled hours riding him. He was trustworthy and just an honest horse, a real babysitter. We never worried about our girls being off by themselves with him.

Dawn often rode alone, and she occasionally went to some waterfalls not far from where we lived on our acreage outside Kelowna. We'll likely hear about adventures we know nothing of in the years to come, just as our parents did. Cassandra admitted to peeing in her dad's thermos one time, so I'm sure we've not heard the last of our girls' stories. My brothers, sisters and I used to sit around the kitchen table when we were all home and make Mom and Dad's hair turn gray with our stories. With some surprise in her voice, Mom would say, "*That's* how that happened." It always amazes me that my siblings and I were never killed with some of the antics we pulled while growing up on our ranch/farm.

Cassandra was always kind to the animals. She loved

them and had a special bond with horses, cats, and her dog, Kelly. She spent hours with the horses and kittens. She adopted a little chick and took it home to her mother's house one time, hiding it in the closet for a while. She then put it in a cage, but one day when the cage was outside something got the chicken. She was heartbroken. Dawn liked the dog too, but she didn't have that special way of communicating with pets that her sister did.

There were some tough years for Cassandra as she progressed through puberty and high school. She always wanted to be a psychologist and I believe would have been very good in that profession. Dawn once told us she wished her sister had lived with us, so Cassandra would not get into trouble. We wished it too and once thought that may happen, but in the end the girls' mother did not agree.

We had some rough days as parents with Cassandra because both Bob and I were raised in homes with strict rules. There were consequences if you didn't toe the line, and sometimes we were hard on her. I know that.

Once I made Cassandra sit down and write out a list of everything she didn't like and those things that she did like about me. I also did the same for her, and we then compared notes and talked about them. It was an interesting discussion.

We have similar personalities, which likely created more conflict. We both are animal lovers and have soft hearts. We also both hide our feelings about certain things. Our relationship has been up and down over the years, so when Cassandra asked if she could call me "Mom," it warmed my heart. Dawn followed with her request a short time later. I had always told both daughters to call me what they felt comfortable with. They simple called me Lynda or their step-mom. I always wished for them to call me Mom so when it happened I felt honored.

Bob was raised in a critical home environment, so it was hard for him to understand the girls in their teens. He had difficulty displaying emotions except for his temper. As a result he had a hard time dealing with his daughters until much later in their lives. He could have maybe complimented them and praised them more often, but praise was hard for him. Criticism he knew how to pass on in large quantities. I would like to think I played a role in my husband's learning how to laugh and interact with his kids. They did say so once. Babies love my husband now and will reach out to him when they meet him for the very first time. He interacts with children differently than he used to.

I'm not proud of it, but I'm probably the only person who ever spanked our oldest daughter. Although she may not know, it hurt me far more than her. In hindsight I would have done things differently. We had gone for a holiday and I am certain she felt her mother's feelings were being hurt just by being with us for two weeks. She acted out, making everyone's lives totally horrid until it was just too much to bear. It takes a long time to make me angry, but I must admit, I lost my temper. After I spanked her, we both cried, and she was upset for some time while we were driving to the next campsite. We hugged and had a pretty good trip the rest of the time. She never did act out like that again.

My girls did have a healthy respect for me because I did follow through with my promises, even if it was doling out punishment. I had to smile one time when Cassandra told me I could never tell her what to do because I wasn't the boss of her. I simply looked at her and said, "Where are you right now? This is my house and in my house I am the boss, so yes, you will do what

I tell you here." She never brought up the subject again although she did tempt me a few times and we did on occasion have words, but I love her to the moon.

Once on a camping trip, I opened my little girls' eyes to new experiences. They had never showered before or skinny dipped in a stream. It was just us girls, but they were properly shocked that people did these things. We camped out and slept in a tent and had great fishing experiences although we didn't catch many fish. To this day, our favourite song is "Fishing in the Dark."

We went to many different camping areas in the Kootenays and enjoyed nature at its finest. There were fires in the Okanagan that year. On one occasion we were evacuated from a campsite and ended up leaving the area early. We made the executive decision to take our girls away from the forest. We did not want to jeopardize their safety, so off we went to Barkerville, a quaint little ghost town in Northern British Columbia where you step back in time. We panned for gold, hiked around the town, watched a great play in the theatre, and saw the hanging tree. It was fun and we all enjoyed our time there.

My old car broke down on that trip unfortunately. I had

a good friend, an old work colleague, living close by. He came to our rescue by organizing a rental vehicle for the balance of our trip. In the end we spent a great deal of money for the rental and getting my car back home. The car needed some extensive motor work which we hadn't counted on too, but all was worth it in the end.

Another year we went to my childhood home for Tish's wedding. I bought the girls matching dresses with different colored hats. All of the adult aunties were wearing hats to the wedding. The girls hated them but they sure were cute! It was the only time I got to dress up my little girls. When we were growing up, my mother had us in matching outfits for church, and I guess my thought was we could do so for my sister's wedding. It was probably the only time they ever wore matching dresses, and they sure weren't very happy about it.

Following the wedding celebrations several of us went for a trail ride in the wilderness on horseback. It was a great trip. The girls had fun riding a little Shetland pony called Thunder. He made a name for himself as the best little pony around. He really looked after the little ones. The neighbors next to my dad's farm (where I grew up) bought him for their children and Thunder went from there to my brother for his little ones to ride. The little pony ended up giving rides to disabled children in his twilight years. He was very special and loved by many, young and old.

While on that same trip, we stayed in an old log cabin that was rumored to have belonged to a horse thief many years ago. It was in a beautiful location set way back in the forest near a river. The cabin was well built as were the corrals. The area was sheltered with lush tall grass. There was a rack of moose horns in the dirt basement of that old cabin that were so big they must have built the house over top of them. It definitely would have been a challenge to get them out as there was only a trap door to the basement. Sad to say a few years after we were there a terrible flood swept through the area and took the cabin away. We are blessed to have experienced the beauty of that spot prior to the flood.

I also had a rather nasty fall on that trip. The horse I was riding was not "rider friendly." She was spoiled. After lying down in the stream I tried to cross, she threw herself over backward going up the river bank. I injured my leg, and it was black and blue for weeks. I was thinking we should have stood on her head while she was in the stream. My tack, including the saddle and everything in the saddle bags, was soaking wet and muddy. My husband rode the horse after that, and she nearly took his head off on a tree branch. She definitely was not a child's horse like Thunder and not one that was ever welcome on any other family horseback ride.

On a later trip with my dad we rode into the Kakwa Lake area southwest of Grande Prairie, Alberta. The girls had their own horses by that time, but it turned out to be a bit of a disaster where they were concerned. Dawn had a run away with her little Frosty. Another horse had started to buck and the rider was thrown, which frightened the little horse. Off he went. As I mentioned earlier, horses have a "fight or flight" instinct. Our eight-year-old daughter was screaming at the top of her lungs. Of course, that made the situation even worse. The poor little horse must have thought the world was ending. Dawn did very well and hung on even though she was frightened out of her mind. I tried to stop Frosty but couldn't. Bob managed to catch him before we had a real wreck. Later Dawn said to me, "It was kind of fun, and I quit screaming because I think it scared him." Dawn then rode on the wagon with Grampa. She must have gotten a taste for speed though, because in her teens, Dawn rode horses *very fast* while barrel racing with her high school rodeo friends. She also did goat tying and pole bending.

We had some fun times on that afore-mentioned horse trip, but the girls weren't really keen on longer rides. It was cold and wet for part of the time, and they were citified after all. Living on an acreage is far different from being in Northern Alberta on a ranch or in the bush. Our girls weren't hardened to the western way of life although they got to experience the joy of spending time with horses and knew what was involved in taking care of them. Bob and I had both grown up with horses. There was every reason to make sure our daughters enjoyed being around them as we started a performance horse breeding program. Before we moved to our acreage, we lived in one of the suburbs. We boarded our horses at a friend's acreage just out of town, and we took our girls on many rides into the nearby Myra Canyon. We spent hours riding those beautiful trails with all of us enjoying those trips. One time our ride was cut short as Bob was on call and received a page when we were on the canyon floor. It was a quick trip out and off to work he went again.

The Myra Canyon was badly burned in the Okanagan fires in 2003 and will never be the same. I was fortunate to hike that canyon with my first husband. We walked over all of the train trestles and through the tunnels. They were amazing, and I marveled at the engineering that had gone into their construction, especially given the era in which they were built. Riding horses in the canyon with Bob and our daughters afforded us the opportunity to enjoy the canyon from a different angle.

Dawn came to live with us when she was fifteen. It was great. She spent weekends with her mother but became quite angry with her mom when left alone some of those weekends. Because of that conflict, boyfriend issues, and hooking up with the "wrong crowd," she ended up running away one afternoon to a town about two hours south of us. When I say "wrong crowd" I use the term loosely as I do not believe there is such a thing. There sometimes are misguided youth who tend to get into trouble, but that does not mean they deserve to be labeled. Our daughter left a note to say she was going to a friend's grandmother's house in the northern part of the province.

Of course, this happened when Bob was out of town

for a couple of days. Therefore I had the dubious pleasure of trying to locate Dawn before she got hurt or into trouble. Before I took the car and headed north, I started calling her friends. I tracked down a couple of them and was able to locate her. I could not talk to her as she had no phone but left a message with her friend to call me. She was, in fact, not in the north, but the southern part of the province.

At first I was very angry and then became worried as she was not worldly and was being manipulated by her friends. She had cashed savings bonds and used the money to buy a car and rent an apartment. Dawn's "friends" helped her spend all of the money.

I did convince Dawn to let me come and talk with her. She would not talk with her dad or mother. She and I sat in her cold apartment and talked for some time. Bob and I had refused to sign for Dawn and her friend to have power or a phone. Both girls were under age and quite scared, but they were determined to stay there. Our daughter ended up being gone for about two weeks until the money ran out. She and her girlfriend were pretty resourceful, though, I must say. They procured an extension cord and had it plugged into an outlet in the hall. They had an electric frying pan and were stealing power to cook their meals. The girls went to bed early because they had no lights. It was a good lesson, but when the money was gone the girlfriend went home. Bob and I went to visit Dawn when she agreed Dad could come. We brought her home that day lock stock and barrel. Dawn insisted she was not going to live at the acreage with us though, and went to live with the friend she ran away with.

Lessons for divorced or divorcing parents... At this juncture I would like to say one thing to all divorced parents. If you have issues with your ex-partner keep them between the two of you. As I previously mentioned, do not put your children in the middle. It is not fair to them and will affect their entire lives. It is difficult enough for grown adults to deal with the break-up of their parents or each other, let alone for their youngsters. There is little reason that there cannot be peaceful resolutions to issues involving children and their separated parents. Using children as pawns in a marriage break up is just wrong. Children have no control over what their parents do, and if you are a bitter partner, then everyone suffers. Revenge is not sweet when your children are hurt in the process.

My parents divorced after being married for thirty-four years but they kept their communication lines open and both attended functions whether it was weddings, christenings, family gatherings, or any grandchildren's events. I am so grateful for this as our family is very close, and even now when I see my dad, he asks how my mother is doing. My parents are both well into their eighties. Dad is with his second wife, and my mother is in a senior's residence.

I have quite a number of friends and family who divorced and are maintaining a tolerant relationship with their former spouse for the sake of the children. It is a healthier way to raise kids given the circumstances. Being bitter hurts everyone but particularly the children. It is not their fault the parents could not stay together.

There is another positive reason for getting along: children are less apt to pit one of their parents against the other to get what they want.

My beautiful grandbabies...I am blessed to have seven beautiful grandchildren!

Cassandra's daughter, Rosie, our oldest granddaughter, spent a few weeks each summer with us at our ranch for several years. She absolutely loved her time on the ranch with us. We emailed each other almost every day after she left. She was so cute. Rosie has always loved music and once told me she "had left the building," just like Elvis did. Rosie loves animals and is so much like her mom. She was always telling rather than asking about how things worked or should work. She was such a sweet little girl and has turned into a lovely young woman who has a shining future.

Mae, her younger sister, once wanted to play hide and seek. When Rosie went to hide, Mae made a map. She said, "Gwamma, I need you to help find heh." She then took me into each room where she looked for her sister. Mae would then point to the map and say, "Gwamma, she isn't in hew," and she would cross off one of the rooms with her pencil. When we got to the bathroom, she found her sister in the bathtub. Her comment as she made a big "X" on her map was, "Gwamma, I knew she was hew all the time, wight hew on this "X", see…"? (Out of the mouths of babes come the cutest things.)

That same little granddaughter called butterflies "boo flies." Mae did get to spend some time with us at the ranch when she was a little older with Dawn's step-daughter, Jaime. They had great fun.

Our grandson, Thomas, is a special boy with many physical and mental challenges. He loves the horses and cars and is learning so much about life. We love him and miss him because they live some distance away. Thomas always asks Grandpa Bob how his horse is doing. Dawn rode our horse, Dolly, for many years, and Thomas has claimed her for his own.

We were also blessed with two beautiful step-grand-daughters, Jaime and Raye. Dawn met and married a man with two lovely daughters just as I had, and we are so lucky to have them in our lives. My grandmother always said that children were welcome into our family no matter how they got there. I feel the same way.

Raye presented us with a gorgeous great-granddaughter, who gives us such pleasure. We live some distance away but recently spent some time with Raye and her little family, thoroughly enjoying our visit. Raye has just given birth to our second great-granddaughter. It is a wonderful experience being a grandparent.

Our grandchildren are all great, unique in their own way, and are growing into wonderful people we are very proud of. I am so blessed. I love each and every one of my grandbabies and have experienced many wonderful moments with these young ones. Children tend to keep adults real. The earth and animals we have on our ranch definitely do that but the children hold a special place in my heart.

My friends... Over the years I have made many friends, some extremely good ones, who are still a big part of my life. Others have come into my life and left but were never forgotten. My best friend, Ann, and I have known each other all of our lives. In fact, my dad and mom were the witnesses for her parents when they married. Our folks were good friends too and spent many hours working together in bush camps, partying, and having fun throughout our growing up years.

Needless to say, Ann and I spent many hours together. We are more like sisters, and I dare say that I am closer in some ways to her than most of my siblings because of our age difference if nothing else. There are few people who can say they've literally had a friend for life. I have some other long-time friends that are very special to me as well but none as dear. Both Ann and I have had near death experiences in the past few years, and we have come to appreciate our love for life and each other even more.

We grow apart from friends for different reasons. One of you may move or end up with other interests, and it seems there is never as much time for the friend that lives farther away. "Out of sight, out of mind" is the saying that rings true in that situation. Also we are naturally drawn to people who have the same interests. Bob aptly put it when he said, "We have many acquaintances in our lives but very few genuine long term friends."

As we go through life, we find out who our true friends really are. Changing life partners certainly affects your circle of friends. Although it is a good thing, there are few friends who can remain loyal to both people in a failed marriage or relationship.

The friends I made in school drifted away as we made our way into the world, married, moved or had children. Some of us stayed in touch for a while, and I have reconnected with many of them twenty-eight or more years later upon moving back home. These friendships are great as we have much to talk about now that we have lived life, loved, had children, and pursued careers.

Friends I made through work stayed there when I moved on. Unfortunately, it was too hard to maintain those relationships. We are still friendly whenever I contact them, but that communication doesn't go both ways; therefore, it's much too hard to maintain the connection. I have much more appreciative friends in my immediate circle.

There are a few I do need to talk about. June and I have been friends since we took our nurses training so many years ago. Her life has been quite different from mine in many ways, but we do keep our friendship no matter what. We live a province apart but she was raised in a ranching/farming community as well, so we have a great deal in common.

June continued with her nursing career and now works at a home for the aged, where she is able to show the deep compassion she has for the elderly and people in general. We know each other well, inside and out, and are almost physic in our ability to know when there is something wrong or bothering the other. She has been through a divorce, raising children on her own, having to start over, health issues that caused her to alter her path in life, and family crisis. We have those things in common as well. I love her and she is an inspiration as are so many others in my life.

I've had some great male friends over the years as well, but they come and go. Most often nowadays they are part of a couple. When I was younger, there were often guy friends who looked out for me and were there when I needed a shoulder to cry on or help with something. Our friendships went both ways but often fizzled out when one or the other of us found a new partner.

I have one very special male friend who has been there for me and vice versa for over forty years. We met T when Mark and he played fastball. It was a fun league, and the wives kept score, cheered them on, and often went out of town to tournaments. So, hanging out after the games, T and his wife Lola became fast friends of ours.

After Mark and I split, this couple remained close to me. When Bob came into my life, they welcomed him with open arms, and there wasn't a week that went by when we didn't spend time with these friends, playing cards, having dinner, or just hanging out with our kids. To this day T is like a dear brother, a true friend in every sense of the word, not only to me, but to my husband as well. (I will explain about Lola further into my story.)

We have some long-time friends from horseback riding days and from Bob's time with the RCMP. Those people are very special to us as well though we don't talk or visit often. We watched our children grow up and spent much time together. Their children call us Aunty and Uncle which means a great deal, especially to me.

Once when six of us were riding our horses on a trail some distance from town, one of our friends suffered a bad fall from her horse. She fractured her collarbone. Bob rode our awesome little American quarter horse, Peppy, at a trot for about seven miles to get a vehicle to rescue her. I subsequently cared for her little girls, especially the baby, until she was able to do that her-self. I was in later years able to be there for their oldest daughter and help her through a rough time. I am so glad to have been there for her.

And that's what friends are for. When I was asked to do the makeup for these "little" girls' weddings, I was thrilled. What an honor! I was unable to help the oldest with her wedding or even attend her wedding, though, as I was in a body cast at the time, but you will learn about that later.

After moving to our acreage near Kelowna, we met and became good friends with the folks next door, Maurice and Belva. They had a son, Reese, who got the German measles when he was three, and he was left with serious brain damage. As the years progressed, Reese became more disabled and began having gran mall seizures. When the doctors were tweaking his medication, he could have up to one hundred seizures per day. His parents remained forever dedicated to their son's care. His mother was away from him for only nine days of his entire life, at which time she was in hospital for a surgical procedure.

Each day that wonderful lady would walk with her son

around their property several times. Belva provided him with much needed exercise and stimulation with these outings. She also acquired a mini zoo for him over the years, and he took pleasure in seeing, petting, and being among the little animals. Often we would join them for their walk or just visit across the fence. Reese and Bob formed a special bond. He had a limited vocabulary, but he and Bob still teased one another. As time went on, though, he also lost his ability to speak.

He loved music and listened to his tapes for hours. Often we found him playing with wooden puzzles, placing the pieces in the right holes on a board. Life became very challenging for this couple as the husband struggled with his health too. Back surgery kept him from work for a time, and later on when he required time off because he could not work, there were no disability benefits to assist them.

They had another son who was younger and he came to his parents for help when he got married. This son and his wife had a beautiful baby girl. Her grandparents could not have been more proud of their baby granddaughter.

In our regional district we had a clause which allowed a

family member to put a temporary home on the property (the land had to be five or more acres in size). Our friends purchased a mobile home and set it up at the west end of their five acres just south of our place. They spent hours and a lot of cash fixing up this home for their son and subsequently also co-signed for vehicles loans to help the children start their lives together.

As time passed a rift developed between the son, his wife, and his parents. The result was devastating. The son and his wife kept their baby girl away from her grandparents. They moved, leaving behind debt and emotional destruction. This incident was heartbreaking, and hard as they tried, Maurice and Belva could not fix the relationship with their son. They did not see their granddaughter ever again.

Their house was like a shrine with pictures of the granddaughter in each and every room. My girlfriend had a collection of figurines and dolls she was saving for her granddaughter in the hope that someday they would have her back in their lives.

The many small exotic animals and birds that our friend kept for Reese eventually became her escape. When Reese was sleeping, Belva would spend time with the animals. The neighborhood children loved to stop by as well, our own girls included. There were miniature goats, a donkey, a pot-bellied pig named Charlotte, and a chinchilla. There were peacocks, hens, and other exotic birds of every different color, shape, and size you could imagine. Belva loved the children coming by although she often had to send them home, for they would have stayed and played with the animals forever had she let them.

These friends of ours loved our dog Jake. Jake would help herd the cows, but he herded them from our side of the fence. Our friends got a kick out of Jake and whenever we were away, there was no doubt he would be well cared for by our neighbors.

Maurice and Belva lobbied the government and agencies they dealt with regarding their son in an effort to permit them to stay home and care for the boy rather than placing him in a facility. They were told many times that he should be in a home for "such children." Respite care did not work, because Reese would not tolerate it. He just could not be away from his parents. As much as you can say he would have adapted, or they should have done something differently, the fact still remains they were his parents, and they chose to care for him. As they said, there was no one who would care for him the way they could, and having him sedated just for the caregivers was not an option. As a result their burden was heavy.

Mr. Latimer, a Saskatchewan farmer, took the life of his disabled daughter. We had several conversations with Maurice and Belva about Latimer's case because of Reese's disabilities. Maurice actually said one time that he might commit that crime if ever there came a time when the only option was placing their son in a facility. He said he would also take his own life so his family would not go through what Mr. Latimer's family endured. We did not take him seriously.

After Bob and I moved to Northern Alberta, our friends' lives deteriorated even more. Maurice became ill; Belva developed arthritis in her feet, making it very painful for her to walk; and Reese's condition worsened. We kept in touch, writing notes and calling each other occasionally. We visited whenever we could, which was a few times each year. They did come to see us briefly on a road trip they took the summer after we moved. We had a very enjoyable visit with them, especially since they hardly ever left home or travelled.

We developed a close relationship with these friends, not only because they were our next door neighbors, but because we walked with them, visited over the fence, and came to know them inside out. I guess you could say we walked a few miles, maybe not directly in their shoes, but certainly beside them while they were in theirs.

Our move to the north and a new career... After Bob retired from the police force he had worked with a colleague awhile before we decided it was time to move. We left British Columbia, our friends, daughters and Bob's parents, and moved to Northern Alberta, where I was raised. We were still following our dreams and raising beautiful performance horses, a passion we both shared. Being too young and too broke to retire, Bob went to work in the oil industry for my brother while I pursued a career as an Independent Consultant with Mary Kay Cosmetics.

I really did not enjoy working with women, and I have always been quite a Tomboy, so it is ironic that I chose a career in cosmetics. However, I found the business plan with Mary Kay far and away above any other home based businesses I have ever encountered. And working with women in this setting is totally different than in most businesses.

I still mentor and encourage self-development, but in this business women move up as far and fast as they wish while being their own boss. I love teaching, sharing my knowledge of the business, and of course, seeing the growth in women. Watching women become the best they can be is heartwarming and exciting. I have seen women come into this business who were afraid to stand and say their name, and within a short time their self-confidence and self-esteem have risen to the point where they want to share for as long as you will let them.

Many ladies whom I would likely never have met except for this business have become my friends as well as my customers.

The successful women at the top of Mary Kay Cosmetics will tell you they would give up the diamonds, cars, travel and other prizes, but not the self-confidence, personal growth, friends, and business knowledge they have gained along the way.

Celebration on achieving status as an Independent Mary Kay Sales Director

Mary Kay was disappointed in women's lot in business, and she wisely put together a marketing plan that is un-paralleled in any other company. The success of Mary Kay and the global empire she built speaks for itself. The Mary Kay marketing plan is studied at Harvard University and many other colleges and universities. The company is built on core values: putting God first, family second, and career third. Mary Kay was once interviewed on *60 Minutes*, a television show in the 1960's and 1970's. She was put on the spot by the interviewer who suggested she was using God to further her business. Her reply was that she hoped God was using her to help women be the best they could be. Mary Kay believed "when you put God first, your family second, and your career third, everything seems to work. Out of that order, nothing much seems to work."

Mary Kay Cosmetics is currently a family owned business with no debt serving over thirty-five markets throughout the world and has been in business for over fifty years. The company is environmentally conscientious, does not engage in animal product testing, and has a company charity that supports community women's shelters and women battling cancer.

All of these reasons drew me to pursue a career with Mary Kay. How I began this business was rather interesting. I have a friend who was needing just one more team member to become an Independent Sales Director and earn the use of her first Mary Kay car. She had introduced me to the products just a few years before, and I loved what they did for my skin. I knew how important this promotion was for my friend and agreed to sign on. My comment to her was: "I will never sell, though, so don't expect me to do anything with the business".

At that time in my life I wore lipstick occasionally, mascara because I am blonde and you cannot see my lashes unless I do, and I also used the skin care products.

My friend needed me to assist her later with a trade fair. I balked but agreed to help her out. I said, "What if someone asks me a question?" I would never have an issue if someone asked me a question concerning topics I was familiar with. I could speak to a crowd of four hundred people or more about insurance and not have difficulty, but I knew very little about cosmetics. She told me to smile and just ask ladies to enter their names for her basket draw. If they asked a question I could not answer, I was to take their number and she would call them.

After the trade show was over, my friend handed me twenty-eight names of ladies who entered that draw and asked if I would call them. She had over three hundred names and could not get to them all. So I discouraged all of the twenty-eight ladies from having an appointment with me, except for one. I had any number of excuses for them not to meet with me. Finally the one lady said to me, "Am I not entitled to a free facial? Do you have the kit?" Of course I had to say yes, and yes I did have a kit. She said, "Well, bring that big girls' toy box over and we can play with it!" Oh my word! What to say next… I agreed to go to her house with the kit.

I drove by that lady's house four times on the day of our appointment. I thought maybe if I tossed the kit on her lawn and told her to call me when she was done, that might work. Then I told myself, "Okay gal, you are a woman of your word so get after it." I drove into her yard and skirted my way around the refuse to the front door. Now remember I was fine with making a speech about insurance in front of many people, riding a horse for hours on end or just hanging out at my little ranchette, not talking about cosmetics or skin care. I got to the door, and wouldn't you know it? She had a friend join her.

There was no kitchen table, so we had our session at the coffee table. I set up for the facial and we began. Now in those days we had a flipchart. There were pictures on one side for the customer to see and follow, and the other side had scripts for the Independent Beauty Consultant. Well, I read and they did, for two whole hours. I now do an entire skin care party with up to eight or ten ladies in about forty minutes.

At any rate we finally finished, and I was amazed they looked so great! I wasn't quite sure how that happened. One of the husbands came in about that time. This lady and her husband were bikers. There were several "hogs" in the driveway when I drove in, which was another reason for my reluctance to go to the door. I wondered if maybe some of the people that lived there had been involved in auto claims at our office and hoped there had been a great end result.

The thought crossed my mind that my husband didn't even know where I was. I might not come home. I wasn't that afraid but did hope I had never denied any claims concerning this man. As it turned out all he could see was his lady, so I didn't have to worry. She looked really good, and he told her so. I firmly believe that was the first time he had ever said anything like that to her. She lit up like a candle. She was so excited.

The only thing I sold that day was an eye pencil because neither of the ladies could afford to purchase anything, but I had my eyes opened in a big way. I realized that this business is about making women feel great! It was an "a-ha" moment for sure. I sent a card to the lady when her birthday came around. She called to thank me, saying it was the only one she had received.

When some ladies at work found out I had a beauty kit, they wanted to see what was in it too, so I found myself placing a couple of orders to purchase product. My Independent Sales Director came with me to an appointment a number of miles out of town to help with a class. That is what we called our appointments then as we teach skin care. I still was very uncomfortable with my presentation but obviously had an impact on the group, as I signed my first recruit at that appointment. She is still a member of my team some twenty years later.

I continued to do a few appointments but mostly took guests to our meeting nights where Independent Sales Directors did the presentations. I learned by watching and took some workshops where I learned more about the business and working with the product. I even started to wear some color myself after a lady said, "You sell the product and you don't even wear color?"

I experimented with eye color shortly after that incident when Bob and I went for dinner with several other couples one evening. There were four of us gals who had birthdays in the same month, and we had decided to celebrate together. So blue being my favorite color, I decided on blue. We had three different shades of blue at that time. You can imagine what took place next. I used them all. My friends must have been chuckling the whole night, but no one embarrassed me. I later learned how to work with color, particularly after the manager with the insurance company told me I should be wearing makeup to help me look more professional. He was right.

After we moved to our new home in Northern Alberta, I got serious about my career in Mary Kay, and told my father I was going to earn the use of a car with the company. He just said, "Well I hope you do." You understand this man had watched me grow up and knew I had never been a "girly girl," so he had a hard time seeing his little girl as a makeup engineer.

When the car arrived, I called Dad to say it was here. I told him the make and model and Mary Kay would pay a portion of the registration and insurance. He didn't believe me at first, so once I explained the car program to him, he was my first passenger. He definitely was excited for me then.

I have a few funny experiences with my Mary Kay journey. Early in my career, I attended a lady's home to give her a facial, and when I put my bags down, both my bags and I were surrounded by twelve ferrets. They were running in and out of the bags, and she asked if maybe she should put them away, as a couple of them were biters. Oh my! Yes, was my reply, of course. She put them in their cage and when I turned to set my bags on a chair, the biggest chameleon I ever saw was right there on the chesterfield. Good grief! I started to wonder if she had snakes too. I am very fearful of snakes.

Another time we were at a conference on the twelfth floor of the host hotel. My mother was with me when the fire alarm went off. We had to take the stairs in our pajamas. We got to the main foyer to find out it was a false alarm. It was suggested maybe there was someone who just wanted to see all of the Mary Kay ladies without their makeup and in their pajamas at two A.M.

We all have an inner need for acceptance and recognition for our accomplishments. I always thought I didn't need recognition but praise feels good. I have earned a number of diamond rings and so many prizes and gifts from the company just for doing my "job."

If you don't have someone in your corner who will give praise for a job well done, you should perhaps find that person or persons.

The tough stuff! Now strap yourself in as you are about to experience some of the tough stuff I have encountered along my life journey.

Just to recap to this time in my life; I had a wonderful childhood with some minor bullying at school, but nothing I didn't learn to handle; was raped when I was seventeen; lost some family, aunts and uncles when I was young; then my grandfather, followed by my grandmother; watched my parent's marriage of thirty-four years dissolve and then my own; lost love and found it again; lost my career; had much sadness over the loss of special animals in my life; then a year of deaths with just one loss after the other, ten in total.

I was strong for everyone through that year and set my own sadness on a back shelf because I was the "Smile of the week!" I have always maintained an outward positive image, and managed to smile through almost anything and everything. In 2001 there was one death after the other from close friends to family and even one special mare that died on Mother's Day.

Then came the devastating experience of SUICIDE.

The loss of three dear friends... Also in 2001 we called our friends, Maurice and Belva to ask if they would care for Jake, our old dog, while we were in their area for Christmas. By this time Jake was pretty old and arthritic. It was a cold winter in Northern Alberta, and we did not want to leave him alone at our ranch. He was still able to travel and liked to be with us. I sensed some hesitancy on our friend's part to have Jake stay with them, so I said it was okay, we could make other arrangements, but Belva told me they would look after him.

When we arrived at our friend's home, I noticed how cold the house was. Reese slept the entire time we were there. The animals and birds had all been sold at auction or been given away. Our friends appeared to be preoccupied but said Jake was welcome to stay with them. The dog was not keen to stay, but he seemed to settle down some before we left.

In the few days that followed, we called to check on Jake. There was no answer. We left messages but weren't overly concerned when they weren't returned. We knew our friends would have called had there been a problem with Jake.

On December 29th we arrived at Maurice and Belva's home to pick up our dog. Jake was waiting at the gate and immediately started to whine when he saw me. I put him in the truck before we went inside to visit with our friends. We spent several hours with them, talking about the past and what their plans were for their son. We could see they were starting to have serious issues in caring for him. Reese was thirty-four by then, and he was very quiet and asleep most of the time. They told us they were looking into placing him in a facility.

While we were saying our goodbyes, Maurice sat dejectedly by himself on the stairs. I could tell he was very depressed and I said to him, "A new year is on the way. You are special and so many people love you. I know things are hard right now, but it will get better." He said, "I'm not of any use anymore," or something along those lines. I assured him that he had so much to give and that we loved him.

Belva kissed my husband on the lips when she said goodbye, something she had never done before. She was sobbing in my arms as she said goodbye to me. She told me it felt like she had lost her husband.

It was very hard leaving them, and I was crying too as we drove away. I told Bob we needed to call them every day if necessary until they got past this bad time.

We then stayed with other friends in the Okanagan that evening on our way back home. Jake continued to be upset, and when we let him out in the morning he messed himself on their deck. I had never seen Jake behave in this manner before. We cleaned up after him, apologized to our friends, and headed home.

New Year's Eve we spent the evening with my family celebrating the coming of the New Year. There was a phone call from Bob's mother. My in-laws were very close with Maurice and Belva as well. Mom H was upset and crying. She said my girlfriend and her son were dead but did not know about the husband. At first I could not believe it and am crying even now as I write this on the fourteenth anniversary of their death. I was nearly inconsolable. The following day we received news from other neighbours to tell us our good friends had taken their son for his usual walk, or so it was assumed, and then took him into their motor home. They always went for hamburgers on Saturdays so going into the motor home would have seemed normal. Our friends than proceeded to overdose their son, then lay down on the bed one on each side of him with the gas turned on. Another neighbor found them some time later that day. When the autopsy was done, it showed they died at about 10:00 A.M. on the 30th, the same time Jake had his accident on the porch. You may believe what you want, but I feel my dog knew what was going on. I only wish he could have told us. It likely would not have changed the outcome because they obviously were determined to end it all.

In hindsight though which is always 20/20, the signs were there. As in all suicides there is guilt and remorse for those who remain behind and who are close to the ones who died. "Why didn't we get it?" "Could we have saved them?" "Would they have done it if we had confronted them?" All those and many more thoughts and questions cross your mind.

We were the last ones to see them alive. Because we were a close knit neighborhood, we spoke with several other neighbors and friends who knew them. We did not go back to attend the memorial service to say our goodbyes, which I realized later was a mistake. My husband said, "We just saw them and that is the way we should remember them."

Their suicide note indicated they had not wanted to see another Christmas. Their original intent was not to live through Christmas, but they had waited until after we were gone.

Our daughter, Dawn, also has a special son, and she wrote a beautiful poem which she read at their service. We were very proud of her. Our dear friends had given her such hope over the time before their death, and they encouraged Dawn to always care for her son. They gave her strength to deal with our grandson's issues as they had for their son.

I still to this day cannot imagine having the conversation that led to their suicide and taking their son's life, albeit he had no quality of life other than being with his parents who loved and cared for him. Both parents had health issues and would not have been able to care for him in the near future. That, along with financial hardship and the estrangement of their son and his family, especially their granddaughter overwhelmed them. They hit the wall and felt they had no other way out.

In the days and months that followed, we heard all kinds of stories about them and much criticism of the choice they made. The story was newsworthy and went to a national level. It was hard to hear people saying things such as: "They surely would not have gone to heaven." "There were other options available for them." "They should have sought help." They were beautiful souls and yes, God had a place for them with Him. It is not our place to judge!

We walked many a mile beside them, and I defended them on many an occasion following their deaths. They were the kindest most generous and loving people. They did believe, although I know they questioned their faith. I miss them terribly to this day.

"The moment that you died my heart was torn in two,

One side filled with heartache, the other died with you.

I often lay awake at night, when the world is fast asleep,

And take a walk down memory lane, with tears upon my cheeks.

Remembering you is easy, I do it every day,

But missing you is heartache that never goes away.

I hold you tightly within my heart and there you will remain

Until the joyous day arrives, that we will meet again."

Unknown

No matter what anyone says it takes courage to actually carry out a plan such as this. They were normal people who were faced with what they felt were unchangeable and insurmountable circumstances. They also felt their son was vulnerable to a society which would hide him away in a place where he had no quality of life and where he would be treated in a manner that was unacceptable to them. Recently the right to die issue has surfaced again. A young woman in Oregon had an inoperable brain cancer and chose to end her life before the worst happened. I believe each circumstance is different, and it will be very difficult for the law makers to decide where to draw the lines on assisted suicide.

We go through life having crises. It is how we deal with each of them and how we move from that position of crisis that makes us who we are. The change for me was the loss of our dear friends. Up to that point I thought I had everything under control. I had done some crying and was sure I was moving on.

Belva and I had celebrated our birthdays together many times. Hers was on the 15th of January and mine on the 23rd. On her birthday the following month, I found myself standing in the middle of my living room crying, not knowing what I had done that day. I am a very strong individual and that feeling of overwhelming sadness was really frightening. I had the good sense to call my doctor. He referred me to a man who specialized in grief counseling. I told my doctor there was no need for medication before my appointment with the counsellor.

When I met with the counsellor he was very kind and welcoming. His office was warm and unassuming if an office can be considered that way. He asked me how I was doing. "Fine," was my reply. Being the smart man he was, he simply asked me to tell him about my life over the last year. I was doing pretty well until I got to the suicide of my friends. I immediately turned into a puddle. Once I had cried the buckets I needed to, we talked about the fact that Maurice and Belva had said their goodbyes and *we* had not. We expected to see them again and not be the last people on earth to ever have the pleasure of their company. We talked about letting go, saying goodbye, building a shrine, or doing something meaningful in their honor. He asked what my safe place was and with little difficulty I was able to tell him. Being with nature on my ranch with the animals was what gave me pleasure and peace. I also love gardening and growing beautiful flowers. I went away from that appointment onto a journey of self-discovery, of knowing my safe place, and working through my grief.

I realized very quickly I had nor grieved sufficiently for any of those friends and family I had lost that year and before.

I also came to the understanding that our friends who committed suicide had made a decision, perhaps not the right one for everyone else around them, but it was their choice. We likely could not have altered that decision either. The result of their choice impacted many people and was a road of no return for them. They knew their plan the day we visited with them and they said their final goodbye. We were not given the option of telling them goodbye for the last time because they were not prepared to share their intentions.

When I visited their graves six months later there were three trees just to the west of where they were laid to rest. The one in the middle was appropriately shorter than the other two. As I stood there crying, I looked up and flying over the cliff nearby was a beautiful eagle. I took that as a sign of peace for my friends and myself. Some of you may believe in such things, others may not. But I did experience a sense of relief as I released the feelings of guilt and sadness.

The next hurdle... In 2004 I made the decision to have my right knee replaced. Being a sports fanatic through the years, I had struggled with knee pain and several surgeries, some minor and one major reconstruction that had me wearing a cast from hip to toe through one very hot Okanagan summer. I couldn't use a coat hanger to scratch the leg inside the cast as there were incisions. Therefore, I spent a very uncomfortable time all the while telling myself that I was not itchy and hot. I also was suffering from severe muscle spasms in the leg as the cast would not allow me to bend it at all. My younger sister can attest to those uncomfortable moments as she came to help out while I was laid up. I've had some great orthopedic care and some not so great through the years. My orthopedic specialist in 2004 told me to wait as long as I could to have the knee replacement, as I was too young. So at his suggestion, I waited until I was using a cane full time.

I remember the pre-operative appointment. I had been through several previous surgeries and never been afraid. One of my aunts was with me at this appointment, and when the doctor went through the procedures with us and told us what to expect, he commented that the worst scenario was that I could die from complications as a result of this type of knee surgery. Up to that point I was only a little nervous, but after he left the room, I teared up and started to cry. To this day I really don't know why that happened, other than perhaps some subconscious premonition.

So on the 13th of December 2004, I underwent the total replacement of my right knee. All was progressing well. I had very little discomfort but had developed a minor topical infection in the incision area, so the doctor kept me there an extra few days. My surgeon had moved prior to my having the replacement done, so the operation had taken place in Calgary, some seven to eight hours from my home. My husband and mother came to the hospital on the 21st of December to retrieve me. On that day I was having considerable pain in the back of my operative knee. Because I was on a blood thinner and because I had not complained of pain at any time since arriving at the hospital, my nurse asked for a venogram prior to my being released. The nurse was definitely my guardian angel as she suspected a clot. Sure enough there was a clot in the popliteal vein. For those of you who do not know, the popliteal is the main vein at the back of your leg which returns blood to your heart. The result was that my blood was pooling in the lower part of my leg with no way to return to my heart.

The official diagnosis was heparin induced thrombocytopenia, a serious life-threatening complication.

What happened next was my horror story. Instead of thinning my blood, the heparin caused the reverse to happen. I was developing clots, and my body was trying to fight this situation by the reduction of platelets. My platelets began to plummet going from the normal 265,000 platelets to 40,000 in just a few days. I developed compartment syndrome. My leg was dying, and I was in danger of losing my life. I had been placed on an artificial blood thinner with a filter also being inserted to prevent clots from reaching my lungs, heart, and brain. This filter was placed in the large vein (inferior vena cava) leading to my heart. On December 26th the decision was made to try a fasciotomy to save my leg or remove it for my survival.

On our way into the operating room, the surgeon stopped the gurney and asked me, "Do you know how serious this is?" I recall having a hard time talking up to that point and know I was hyperventilating due to the pain. Morphine wasn't making a difference anymore. My leg was over forty centimeters in circumference by that time. I recall saying to my doctor, "I think I know, as my husband and mother were crying when they said good-bye just now." The doctor then said, "We may not come out of here tonight, and if we do the chances are really good that you will not have your leg. I need to know how you are doing." I then told him, "I am not going to die. The Lord doesn't want me yet, and I have too much to do. I am not ready to die. You know your job and God will walk us through this so let's go." (That is as close as I can remember it.) The doctor teared up and we went into the operating room. I remember having to fight and make a choice during the surgery. I recall being at the edge and having to decide to fight or let go. It seemed an easy thing to let go and just drift over the edge, but I wanted to live. The next several days are a blur as I fought for my life.

There was a second surgery the day after to remove more of the dead and dying tissue in my leg. After the surgeries there were multiple incisions, but most importantly I did keep my leg. I will be forever grateful to the unnamed donors whose blood and platelets were pumped into me over the next several days. My surgeon came to see me every day just to say hello and see how I was doing. Later the nurses told me he was a changed man after that surgery. He became more personable, had a better bedside manner, and worked more closely with them. I am very grateful to him, his skill, and the powers in play that night. He had my original surgeon, who was out of the city spending Christmas with his family, on the phone throughout my surgery.

A few days after the second fasciotomy, I called Lola, my long-time friend. She and T had split some time before. We had known one another for over thirty years. I had been very clear with both friends about my relationship with each of them. They were like a brother and sister to me, and I would not take sides. She wanted to know why my husband had not called or let her know of my condition. I told her Bob could not tell anyone. He was so emotional during this time. She chose to tell me I could no longer be her friend. She needed me to support her and believed I could not do so while being her husband's friend as well. I was devastated and tried desperately to keep our relationship from dying, but she chose to end it entirely. To this day we have seen each other only once at her daughter's wedding, and she was barely civil. As mentioned before T has remained a wonderful loyal friend to Bob and me.

Lola and I had raised our children together and spent many hours playing and travelling with our families. We had shared intimate conversations about our lives, shed tears over the loss of loved ones and pets, and I valued her as one of my closest friends. She chose the absolute worst time possible to end our long-standing friendship.

Despite that conversation and the odds against me, I made a remarkable recovery, due in large part to my positive attitude, but also to the exceptional care I received, my faith, and the love and care of my family.

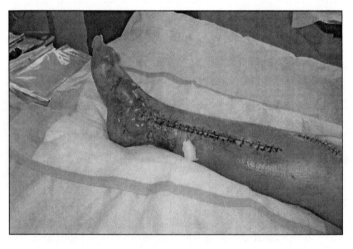

One month after my initial surgery to save my life and leg

I had three toes that were black, a very large blister on my big toe, with another on the baby toe. It was thought at the very least I may lose some toes. However, they all survived. I accidently popped the blister on my little toe while on my way to the washroom one night. I hit the edge of the commode with my toe and the blister absolutely exploded. Both the nurse and I got some of the outgoing debris.

I teased one of my nurses with that blister on my big toe. The blister had a lot of fluid in it and was about the size of a large plum. The doctors and nurses did not want to pop the blister for fear of infection, saying it would be better for my body to absorb the fluid. The liquid inside sloshed a little when I moved my foot. Whenever I heard this particular nurse come into the room, I would wiggle my foot. She would say, "Oh, don't do that, it's gross!" And then we would both get the giggles.

I spent three and a half months in hospital recovering, learning how to manage my wounds and taking phys-iotherapy. I also had to work hard at keeping my spirits up. Physio was done in my bed, as I was not allowed to walk on my leg. My blood levels bounced about for some time until the blood thinner I was able to take was regulated. I subsequently spent several months in a wheelchair, then with walkers, and slowly graduated to crutches followed by a cane. There were open wounds which Home Care nurses, Mom, and Bob had to dress daily for several months. It was a painful yet reflective time. I spent many hours alone. I was immobile and unable to do anything other than think, read, or watch television, and you can only do so much of each.

I have to acknowledge the wonderful nurses, doctors and friends that made my hospital stay so much more bearable. There were two nurses in particular to whom I owe a great deal. One was a male nurse who was a wonderful caregiver and taught me so much about being my own advocate. He also gave me much information about my reaction to heparin, and the resulting thrombocytopenia. He was very diligent where the dressings and resultant care of my leg were concerned. There were many nurses and resident doctors who reviewed my case so I was constantly a teaching patient. I became so knowledgeable, I became the teacher many times. The nurse who requested my venogram was wonderful because of her training, compassion, and dedication. There were many others who gave me exceptional care as well but these two definitely stand out in my memory.

There were friends and family who housed Bob and my mother while they were in the city to visit and support me. Also two ministers stopped by regularly to spend time with me.

A patient in the next bed before I was moved to an isolation room became my friend. She, her husband, their minister and church members were great support as well.

Remembering what my therapist said when I went for grief counseling a few years before my surgery, dwelling on those things that made me happy, really helped. Once I was home by myself, the ability to remain positive and put myself in a good space was extremely important.

My old dog Jake spent considerable time with me even though he was not well himself. He was seventeen years old by this time, but totally dedicated to me. He was good company. I had another special little friend. My neighbor stopped by one day with a tabby grey and white kitten. I will forever be grateful to her for bringing that little cat into my life. Sadie and I spent nine years together, and she gave me such joy. She presented me with several litters of babies. Baby kittens just warm your heart. Sadie actually kissed her babies. I never had a camera at the right time to capture this, but it was special to watch. The moment she became pregnant, the purring started when she was just sitting by herself or even while she was sleeping. Sadie thought she was my protector, and was known to growl at people if I was in bed resting. She likely could have been a formidable foe as I had seen her put the run on dogs she thought were too close to her babies.

My feline friend and protector, Sadie

My shotgun seat rider, Jake, who faithfully stayed by my side to the age of seventeen and a half years old

I also have a great view from my home. I have always loved nature and scenery and captured many a beautiful evening or sunrise with my camera. So living in a home with a beautiful view was definitely a bonus and good for my soul.

Positive self-talk was so important during this time. Never did I believe there would not be a full recovery. I thanked God daily for my blessings and had an attitude of gratitude. I was grateful for all of the good things in my life each and every day, including the caregivers who helped me through this tough time, particularly my husband, and my mother.

I spent a long time with physiotherapy, dressings, and learning how to use my toes and leg again. I remember being so ecstatic about picking up a marble with my toes. I just had to call someone and tell them as I had been diligently working on this exercise for about two weeks. When I called my dad, he was not quite sure what to say. I'm certain he was dumbfounded by my excitement. When I explained how important it was, he simply said, "That's my good little girl."

I am left with many unsightly scars, and I also have to wear a toe to thigh compression stocking every day while I am up. The filter in my inferior vena cava is a permanent fixture. The filter had adhered to the tissue surrounding it so could not be removed. Because of the filter, I have to use blood thinners for the rest of my life. I feel these are a small price to pay for the fact I have my life **and** my leg.

So begins the next chapter of my saga... By the spring of 2008 I was finally able to move around some without a cane. The wounds had healed well.

Bob and I owned a horse that came from wonderful successful barrel racing stock. She was expecting her first baby. Separated from the herd as she grew near to foaling made her quite agitated and lonely, so we brought an older experienced mare into the pen for company. I was on foal watch nightshift, checking for a baby or signs thereof. I still couldn't do much walking especially on uneven ground, so kept watch from a bedroom window while my husband slept.

There was nothing at 3:00 A.M., but by 4:00 A.M. I could see we had a baby. I called my husband from his sleep and off we went to the barn.

Our other horses were next to the foaling pen. The older mare was very agitated and trying to keep them away. Things were a bit "western," so we put the old mare back out with the herd thinking our new mom would have time to bond with her baby. Instead the new mom became very upset and we were concerned she was going to hurt the foal. She was confused so we brought the older mare back in thinking that would settle things down.

Quite the opposite occurred. Our older mare immediately attacked the new mom. It was a very frightening experience. I had witnessed horses fighting before but never anything this violent. My husband was able to separate them, but during the fracas the foal was pushed through the fence into the pasture with the rest of the herd. I quickly crawled through the fence and kept him protected.

By the time Bob removed the older mare, I had the foal partway back through the fence when baby lost his balance. I was standing on the uneven edge of a trail and could not hold him. We both went down with the little fellow partially on top of me. I had immediate pain in my back and called out. (I screamed actually.)

After Bob removed baby and got him settled with his mom I managed to pull myself along the cable fence to the corner of the foaling pen. My husband hurried to the truck which was still at the house. I was in excruciating pain. After getting the truck stuck, we finally made it to the house where I literally crawled into our home. I got as far as the kitchen and couldn't make it any further.

When the ambulance got there the lead hand said she could not get the stretcher through the door into our house. Bob told her our doors were thirty-six inches (normally doors are only thirty inches wide), and there was also another entrance if she couldn't use this one. By this time the morphine they gave me had kicked in and I was feeling less pain. For some reason the attendant insisted I crawl out and climb onto the stretcher. Somehow, I did it.

No back board was used and the ride to the hospital was torture. Once we arrived I spoke with several different medical staff and relayed my story multiple times. When the doctor ordered the x-rays, he requested pictures of my hip and only one of my back. There were signs on the side of my jeans to indicate I had landed on my hip.

No hip fracture showed up on the x-rays, so they sent me home. During the rest of that day and the next two I was home attempting to cope with the pain. On the Monday I called my doctor's office, and he actually answered the phone himself. I explained to him what had happened. He asked what time I could be at his office. "My sister Jean drives a school bus and she could bring me in about nine-thirty," I said. He told me not to stop at reception when I got there but to come straight into his examining room.

After a cursory examination and a couple of questions he said, "I'm pretty sure I know what is wrong. Just give me a minute to call the radiologist. He owes me a favour." When my sister and I arrived at the hospital, there were forms we needed to complete. We then faced some wait time in the x-ray area. I had been standing and sitting, putting pressure on my injured spine for over three hours by this time and was nearly in tears from the pain.

The hospital staff put me on a stretcher at my sister's insistence, and when the CAT scan was done, the technician ran for the radiologist who called my doctor. I had a burst fracture in my lower spine. I was air-lifted to another hospital to see the specialist there as my orthopedic doctor was on his way to Australia. He referred me to the neurologist and said he was one of the best.

The neurologist said, "You are very lucky to have avoided living in a wheelchair," and he put me on complete bed rest with no movement at all. I was log rolled for care and to keep pressure off my spine. And I had to wear the dreaded diapers. When the bed was needed for other acute patients, I was air-lifted to a different hospital where I spent a week. I was then air-lifted back for another week in care of the neurologist.

The x-rays by this time were showing significant progress in healing, so I did not require surgery. I am so grateful for the expertise of the neurologist. He made the right choice in not using the knife as I have healed so well. I was sent home in a clam shell type body cast which I wore for a further five months.

Being sent home was somewhat of a challenge! Bob and I were told I would be air-lifted home due to the nature of my fracture and the fact we live five hours driving time from this hospital.

The discharge nurse had other plans, however, and decided to send me home so she could free up the bed, but she would not arrange a flight. I had no street clothes, no money, or <u>cards</u>, and no one close to come for me. I was also quite ill as I had been given too much medication (morphine) the day before. What a mess!

The discharge nurse refused to help. I was able to arrange a ride with my brother-in-law Doug, after he was finished work. He and my sister Kate live an hour from the hospital. My husband was working and would not arrive until later that night with a five-hour drive ahead of him to get there.

Meanwhile I was put in a wheelchair and set out by the nursing station for over two hours. The directions from the neurologist were to avoid loading my spine for any length of time and recline for longer periods than being up. Sitting was the worst position I could be in. Needless to say I was in considerable pain when Doug arrived, and we still had another hour to drive!!!

I was feeling nauseous and ready to cry from the pain by the time we arrived at Kate's house. When Bob drove me home the next day, we had a very long journey. We stopped several times so I could lie across the back seat of the truck. We were not able to keep my bad leg elevated, and with no compression stocking it turned bright red and excruciatingly painful. The cast specialist at the hospital also did not have the opportunity to check the fit of my cast prior to my leaving the hospital. Subsequently, when I was sitting the cast was putting a great deal of pressure on my legs. I had two baseball size black bruises on my thighs by the time we arrived home. It certainly was another test of my pain threshold and ability to think positively.

Again I was faced with challenge. Not only was there the pain to deal with but long hours alone while I recuperated in bed. Pain medications were again on my agenda along with the body cast. My faithful cat Sadie was again by my side although my trusted old dog had gone by this time. .

One of the most annoying and embarrassing things was not being able to wipe my own bottom. I eventually figured out if I used a pair of long barbecue tongs to hold the paper, it would work. Needless to say, we never used the tongs for anything else and they are now in a landfill.

Eventually after five long months, I was again blessed with the miracle of my mobility and being able to walk.

I got a new puppy, Gus, and we started going for walks in the pasture. I gained strength and more mobility, however by this time I was having problems with my "good" knee. It had taken so much stress during recovery from all of my health challenges. I started walking without a cane or walker and soon began to fall occasionally. My family doctor referred me to the orthopedic specialist again and thus begins the next chapter. The orthopedic surgeon who had operated on my right knee knew my issues going forward.

So in September, 2011, I had my second total knee replacement, the left leg this time. I definitely became my own advocate with the internist when he suggested heparin would not be a problem for me if we used it again. I absolutely refused. I told him, "This is my life we are dealing with here, and I will not be having heparin or any form of it as a blood thinner after the surgery!" I wanted to use the same synthetic blood thinner that was administered after my last surgery when things went so crazy. His reply: "It has to be administered by IV and is very expensive." When I suggested getting another opinion, he was offended. He obviously was not used to being questioned. I contacted my previous internist and he agreed heparin was a drug I should never receive again. He was also concerned about the medication being suggested as an alternative. I relayed that second opinion to the internist that was going to be with me for the surgery. The two internists discussed using the new drug suggested, and we all finally agreed to go ahead with it, albeit reluctantly on my part. There were no guarantees that it would be totally safe for me.

As it turned out that blood thinner did make me extremely nauseous and kept me from doing much physiotherapy. I was only in hospital for a few days before they released me. The physiotherapist was concerned about the bend I had in my operative leg, but because I was able to do all of the physio exercises, there was no delay in my going home.

A month later when I went for my follow up with the orthopedic surgeon, who advised me there was only forty degrees flexion. He said, "If you do not achieve at least ninety to one hundred degrees flexion within the next two weeks I will have to do a manipulation." I asked him exactly what that was. He said, "Well, that is where I bend your leg so your heel touches your bum." *Oh my gosh, I thought what next?* The doctor also said, "Because of your history we will check for blockages first." I definitely didn't want to experience a *manipulation*.

The ultrasound showed a baker's cyst in the back of my left knee joint. A baker's cyst is a painful condition. The cyst is similar to a ganglion. It could be removed, but the risk of infection is high and the cyst would likely return. So after weighing that for all of about ten seconds, I decided with the advice of my physician to try physiotherapy instead. We have an excellent local physiotherapist. At one point he said he must be hurting me. I told him he couldn't make me cry! I am excited to report that we achieved 132 degrees flexion. His goal was 120 degrees; whereas, my personal goal was 130 degrees. How exciting that we reached success beyond even what I was hoping to achieve!

I am finally walking without assistance almost all of the time and boy does it feel good!

There are days that involve pain and discomfort, but on those days I think about so many others who are in much worse circumstance, with days or months to live, or in constant severe pain physically or emotionally, and I push forward. I also focus on how grateful I am to have achieved this much mobility.

Just when I thought things had settled down and the worst things that could possibly happen had, another challenge... While I was recovering from my surgery and still unable to drive, my nephew and his wife had a beautiful baby girl. My sister Jean, who was my driver, asked if we could pick up the siblings of the new baby and take them to see her after my physiotherapy. I said sure. We rounded up the children and off to the hospital we went. My niece was very tired and still in a lot of discomfort but very happy about the birth of her beautiful baby girl. The nurse came to take baby for her first bath, and the children, their daddy and my sister Jean went with them.

This was definitely a special time for the little ones, their dad and Grannie Jean, so I told my niece if she wanted to rest, I would go sit in the lounge or outside the room. She said "No Aunty, I just want to visit with you."

I am so blessed we had that time together. When we left, I hugged her and told her, "I love you". She said, "Thank you for coming, Aunty. It was special for me and I love you too."

"Our children are only ever lent to us.
We never know just how long we will be able to
keep them for.
So kiss them, cuddle them, praise them and hold
them tightly.
But most of all, tell them you love them every day."
Carly Marie

You never know when it is the last time you will see someone. My beautiful niece passed away the following day due to heart failure. I've asked God why. It seems so unfair. My nephew was left alone with three little children to raise. We lost a wonderful young woman, a great mom, a part of our family, and the love of my nephew's life.

Our family is close and we rallied around my nephew and his family, but it is so sad we do not have our niece. One of her last wishes was that her baby would have her blue eyes. Baby is still little as I write this, but her eyes often look blue. My nephew named his baby after his wife, the first name being one they had chosen together and her second name is her momma's. Our nephew is a wonderful daddy and has taken his duty seriously. He left his job to be both mom and dad to his little ones.

Baby was sleeping through the night in two weeks, and he moved his family to my sister Jean and her husband's farm, where the children were able to run, play and just *be* – like all children should. My nephew remained involved with his children, taking a hot dish to lunch day at school, the only dad there. He took it in stride and although he dealt with immeasurable grief, he carried on. I am so proud of this young man.

I cannot say enough about my sister too, what she sacrificed to help her child deal with this situation, and the loving manner in which she cared for him and her grandchildren. She is a wonderful person and had to work hard not only physically, but mentally, while dealing with her own grief as well as trying to maintain the roles of mother and grandmother. It was difficult for her to separate those two roles sometimes. I cannot say enough about my sister's love and care for her son and grandchildren during this difficult time. Her dedication and care was the mainstay of their recovery as a family.

My nephew has since found another amazing woman to share his life and children with.

We will always miss a special young mother who left too soon and couldn't be with her babies while they grew up. Our family's duty now is to keep her memory alive in the minds of her children and help mold them into the beautiful people they are meant to be.

The community in which we live has been generous, caring, and supportive. The saying, "it takes a community to raise a child" is literal in this instance. It has been truly amazing!

I was lucky to care for my nephew's two little girls and sometimes their brother one day per week, but feel it was I who was the biggest benefactor. I love them all and enjoy every moment we spend together. I don't see the children nearly as often now as the two oldest are in school, and the little one is at day home with other children a few days per week.

Their new mom is a great gal. She is a city girl, never married or had children, who has taken on living in the country with three children and a man who wishes to farm and raise cattle. It takes a special person to walk into a situation such as this and learn how to be a mother and wife. She is doing so tremendously well, and I am proud of her.

I also know there is an angel up there watching with

love, who is okay with her husband's choice. She would not want him to be unhappy, and I am very sure she is glad he found a woman who has so willingly taken on her family and is also a great mom. I believe it is harder for a woman to walk into a relationship with a man who has lost his wife to death rather than divorce. With divorce the love is usually gone. In death the man must learn to love two women, one that he must let rest.

Having seen my sister, Jean, deal with this tragedy in her life I need to share the love of sisters with you... We all should have the love and understanding of a sister. I am fortunate enough to have five sisters: three siblings (Kat, Jean, and Tish), one much younger step-sister (Carol-Lee), and my life friend (Ann).

I spend time nearly every week with Ann and still feel our time together is not enough. We have been close all our lives, except for a time when Ann's first husband made sure she was not connected with her friends. He was an abusive man who alienated Ann from friends and family. I am surprised at how many young women there are who allow themselves to be drawn into abusive relationships. I come across them often in my business. Our generation taught our daughters to be strong and independent but it seems there is lack of confidence and self-esteem in too many young women today.

Ann mustered enough courage and strength to leave her husband and go to the local women's shelter. She was very lucky to have done so as her husband took his life later and had intended to take her with him.

Ann and I are both into our second marriage with men who get along extremely well, being much the same in their manners and beliefs, so we comfortably spend time together as couples.

My three biological sisters and I have spent many hours together separately or as family groups with our children and husbands. Our bonds are strong. We have been fortunate to share some of those experiences with Carol-Lee too.

Some years ago we travelled to the mountains with our Dad and rode horseback for a week in a beautiful wilderness setting. Dad says we are still the best outfit he ever took to the mountains. We had a lot of laughs and special moments and saw some amazing country. And to share that experience with our dad was that much more special.

We sisters also spent a weekend together sometime before that trip in a city a few hours away and had a blast. It was the first time as grownups that we had an opportunity to be together without our children and husbands. We learned so much about each other and made some wonderful memories.

We attended a church service in the beautiful old church where a famous hockey player was married. Some kind ladies asked us to join them for a luncheon at a stately old hotel after the service. When we arrived, it seemed rather odd there were no men in attendance, and once the meal started we learned why. We were at the Catholic Women's League annual elections luncheon. When the voting began, we considered nominating Kat for the secretary's position. We instead turned to the lady next to us and told her we probably shouldn't be there. She told us it would be fine if we quietly left. Needless to say, once into the elevator we collapsed into gales of laughter.

In my early twenties I travelled to the east coast of our country with Kat and that trip resulted in a lifetime of unparalleled closeness and memories. We learned about our roots and our ancestors who were raised in those provinces. We met some amazing relatives and other folk with whom I remained in touch for years. I have visited the east coast three more times since then and shared some adventures there with my daughters.

We five sisters and a niece flew to New York recently. We saw and experienced more in four and a half days than most people do in two weeks. What an adventure! There were many laughs, and we opened our world to the beauty of a city I never dreamed of visiting, one that was certainly not on my bucket list. The architecture and history of that city I never expected. A must see and do on our list was a trip to Harlem for a church service. After the service was over, we intended to go to Central Park. There was a definite police presence in the area with roads being blocked off, so we asked what was happening. An officer advised it was the African American Freedom Parade. We just had to see that! On our way to the parade route, we met a local lady who was also going there. She told us more about this all-day event, stating the city only allowed for the celebrations to last until just before dark now, as there had been too many shootings at previous events. Being among the only white people on the street was interesting, and I found myself checking out the crowd to see if anyone was "packing heat." There were many police and prison groups represented in the parade lineup. Oh how interesting were the people! We had so much fun!

We are now planning a trip to Scotland with our husbands. This promises to be wonderful and such a learning experience. Scotland is where our family roots are. The family castle still stands. Who knows what kind of adventures await us there?

Sisters are special. They are great confidants, a shoulder to lean on, and givers of advice in situations where you may need help. They're always there for you in times of trouble.

Our extended family is close enough that we share sister type bonds with our girl cousins as well. I feel very blessed to have them all in my life.

So let's talk about getting older and ageing...

Youngsters cannot wait to grow older. When we're older, many of us wish we were younger. Some people have regrets and wish they could turn back time and have a do-over. We must forgive ourselves for our regrets, what we did or didn't do.

I have always lived life and didn't care about my age, although there have been a few times when age affected me.

Admittedly I went into bars occasionally while under age but was never asked for ID (identification). Ironically, when the age limit changed from twenty-one to eighteen in my province, it seemed I was asked for ID every time, bar employees just doing their due diligence, I suppose.

That being said I have always looked young for my age. Sometimes, actually fairly often, I am mistakenly taken for being younger than my sisters. Kat is six years younger than I with Tish being twelve years younger. Carol-Lee is twenty-four years my junior, so if anyone were to say I look younger than her, we might have a problem.

Good skin care makes a difference along with a sunny outlook on life. As mentioned previously, I was once recognized as "Smile of the Week" in a local newspaper. I don't recall how they chose their "Smile of the Week," but I was well known in the community for many things including my smile.

Another time when age became an issue was when I was approached to become a manager at the insurance company where I worked. Being young and female was detrimental to my being a successful manager at that time. I had the technical skills, but as I mentioned earlier, my supervisor suggested a more professional look would benefit me. He told me to begin wearing suits and makeup. At first I was offended but soon realized he was absolutely right, as I was dealing with employees who had been my peers and some who were much older than I. Looking the part went a long way to giving me credibility and I went on to become a successful manager despite my age and gender. Mary Kay Cosmetics has a dress code for that same reason. It's called dressing for success.

With age comes arthritis and sensitivity to cold, just to name one of the more common health afflictions, thus the flock of snowbirds that head south for the winter to warmer climates to make their lives more bearable. Bob and I have been thinking of buying a fifth-wheel trailer and joining the migration.

We have worked hard to save for our retirement. Unfortunately, as is the case in many people's lives, we were faced with issues that prevented us from building retirement savings. My issue has certainly been physical; many dollars having been spent with not enough coming in while I was ill or incapacitated.

Our beautiful stallion HD Smoke 'n' Color and myself

My husband and I also followed another dream when we raised and showed our beautiful Tobiano, a paint stallion. We incurred a lot of debt to give him a show record, which was further increased by my subsequent illness. We are still working to overcome those resulting financial challenges with only a few years to retirement.

Another fact of life that occurs for many people is taking care of our ageing parents. We do not wish for them to suffer needlessly and most times the caregivers suffer too, all the while wondering, "Did I do the right thing for my parent; could I have done more?"

Our elderly folk need an advocate when they reach those stages of their lives and inability. I am so blessed to have been an advocate for some of the elderly in my family.

One of my cousins said, "The most profound growing up experience is the loss of your second parent. You suddenly realize that you are very much on your own." It is extremely difficult to watch our aging parents struggle with pain and the loss of their independence and dignity.

I wish to cross off more items on my bucket list.

However, I am limited in many things physically. As much as I hate to admit it there are many things I just cannot do. It is frustrating but "if wishes were horses, I'd have a stampede." I still own horses but we don't have enough for much of a stampede!

I applied for early pension to enjoy some fruits of my labor. I paid the maximum into Canada Pension for many years. I enjoyed depositing my first CPP cheque. Now I have the money transferred into my account electronically. The novelty of receiving that first cheque in paper form was worth it!

As we get older little things mean so much more but bother us less and we don't usually take ourselves quite so seriously. Enjoying the little things in life and not letting the small stuff be a burden is so important.

Some of the most important things in life aren't things. One day you will look back and realize the small stuff was just that, and not important. When Irma Bombeck said: *"Dance in the rain and use the good china",* she was so right. Don't wait. Do it now! My mother was an advocate of actually dancing in the rain. We did it many times as children.

Another very important thing I believe is that we never quit learning… I look for something in each day to fill my cup with knowledge, love, or understanding.

So how should we deal with the crises in our lives? I one day realized that there will be crises throughout the rest of my life. I will be faced with challenges such as the loss of my parents and friends, along with disappointment and issues with my own health. My parents are elderly now, both in their eighties, and they both suffer with chronic pain. I spend quality time with them whenever possible. I take care of my mother's affairs for her and visit several times per week. I recently lost an uncle as well as Ann's father. They and my Aunty Evelyn were all in nursing homes. My father is at home still but requires assistance.

Many of the older generation in our family are eighty to ninety years of age and beyond, with a number of them on a slippery slope with health issues. Some of these folks are just plain wearing out and would just like to pass on to the next level in their life's plan. There are also a few for whom there is no quality of life anymore and I wonder what the purpose for their lingering is: Is there some lesson they need to teach us before they go? Only God knows.

I realize that life works in full circle, and in that circle, we are born, move from childhood to adolescence, then adulthood to old age; we then leave this world and another baby is born. We are so very fortunate in our family to have longevity with our parents, aunts and uncles, living into their eighties and nineties. So many lose their parents at a young age. My mother's parents were both gone by the time she was twenty-one years old. Having said that, when there is no quality of life anymore it is a blessing when our loved ones are able to pass away. I know my mom would be happy to go home to be with Jesus and the loved ones who have gone before her.

"You are going to lose people in your life and realize that no matter how much time you spent with them, it will never be enough." Unknown

Even living day to day I realized if you live your life full circle, you are much more fulfilled.

When you put your faith first, family second, and your career third, it all fits. If you put those three things out of order it just does not. These words came from Mary Kay Ash.

For many years all but my career took a back seat. I loved my husband and my family but put God and them on the back burner. I tried unsuccessfully to keep my life in balance. Once I left my chosen career there was a peace and balance I did not know was possible, nor had I realized what was missing. We often allow ourselves to become so *busy* we miss the important things in life.

Depression versus anxiety, fear, sadness, and grief... When we lose loved ones the grief that follows can be overwhelming. So is that grief considered depression? Let's have a look at what depression is.

Merriam-Webster's dictionary defines depression as "a mood disorder marked especially by sadness, inactivity, difficulty with thinking and concentration, a significant increase or decrease in appetite and time spent sleeping, feelings of dejection and hopelessness, and sometimes suicidal thoughts or an attempt to commit suicide."

Despite this definition, I am of the firm belief that sadness or grief is **not** a state of "depression."

A friend once told me I was depressed. Being offended by that remark, I told her, "I am not depressed just very sad!" This was after the losses of friends and family, culminating in the suicide of our dear friends, a total of ten deaths in a period of one year. How could I be anything but sad?

So, was I depressed? It depends on what you think depression means. There are those who would say I was.

The state of depression has carried a stigma with it for many years. If you were depressed you were often shunned, or thought to be crazy. Truth be told, Einstein was diagnosed with depression and look at the brilliance of that man. I have often thought that the brilliant mind borders a fine line between sanity and insanity.

In recent years with more awareness, depression is not the scary place it was when my mother was young. Years ago women were often sent to insane asylums when they had feelings of sadness or anxiety. The form of treatment in many cases was shock therapy. I am so sensitive to electricity that if I wasn't "crazy" before the shock therapy, I certainly would be after. My mother's oldest sister was one of those ladies who ended up in a mental institution for a short time where she received shock treatment not once, but twice! Personally, I believe she was frightened because of feelings she was unable to deal with - but shock therapy?!

Is there a tendency for women who are menopausal to fall into depression? I believe my own mother was depressed when she left my dad after thirty-four years of marriage. She was anxious, fearful of her future, regretful about choices she did or did not make, and feeling very lost. She was also experiencing menopause.

So is depression simply a mixture of all these confusing emotions?

The mind is an amazing thing. Our subconscious can tell us to shut out pain, grief, bad experiences, sadness, fear, and anxiety. Sometimes when my mind did so, it was to my detriment; other times it was definitely beneficial.

I have learned that being able to remain positive in the face of adversity no matter what kind, is so important to your well-being. I also believe that if you can maintain a positive outlook on life all hurdles seem less intimidating.

There will always be times in your life when you feel overwhelmed for any number of reasons. Those reasons might include your children growing up and leaving to make a life of their own, feelings of inadequacy, rejection for whatever reason, fear, pain, grief, loss (this can cover a huge area from the loss of a career to losing a pet or loved one), anxiety or guilt.

There are many people who have cried buckets of tears where no one could see them. They did not share their feelings with anyone for fear of failure and/or rejection. They did not want to feel any more inadequate than they already did.

"Men fear failure, women fear rejection!" What an accurate statement!

When you are in a state of depression, whatever that depression looks like, it can impact your physical well-being in a profound way. When you see depressed people, you will notice that they are often physically unwell too.

"One day she finally grasped that unexpected things were always going to happen in life. And with that, she realized the only control she had was how she chose to handle them. So, she made the decision to survive using courage, humor and grace. She was the Queen of her own life and the choice was hers." Kathy Kinney

In the definition it says that depression often leads to suicide. Although I have felt the impact of suicide, I don't pretend to be an expert when it comes to the subject. I expect there have been occasions when some of you have wondered if the world might be better off without you. Feelings of emptiness or grief that are overwhelming can make anyone desperate. Please talk to someone you trust with your confidences if you find yourself in that place. There are people who care and want to help. If you don't feel there is anyone who can lift you up (and it may be God), then seek out professional help and examine those feelings. There are those who can help guide you. It is important to find ways for dealing with your desperation. I say desperation because it is my belief that anyone who finds themselves contemplating suicide is indeed desperate.

Suicide is final, there is no turning back! There is always something better down the road, regardless of the blackness of a particular place in your life.

> *"Never give up!*
> *Reach inside! Give it all you've got!*
> *As long as you're alive you can keep on trying!*
> *Never give up!*
> *Discover how strong you are!*
> *Don't let anything or anyone bring you down!*
> *Instead be someone who lifts others up by not giving*
> *in and inspiring others with all you've achieved!*
> *Never give up!"* Karen Salmansohn

We all have achieved something in our lives whether it be big or small. Celebrate those achievements and be proud for having accomplished them.

Once again I believe that being grateful for all of the good things in your life is a first step in releasing yourself from black places where you should not dwell. There is always something better even though sometimes you may not believe it. The "something better" might just be comparing your situation to someone else's. For instance I met a lady with no legs and disappearing hands because of her medical condition. I felt so grateful to be blessed with all that I have. That was one of the reasons I reached out to her. I am a compassionate person by nature and believe it is important to give someone a lift up when he or she needs help.

I know my friends who committed suicide felt they had nowhere to turn. They had lost all will to keep trying; however, they did not seek the help that was needed. Never let pride stand in your way when looking for help.

No matter what don't give up!!!

I know I have touched on a delicate subject here. I am far from an expert in the field of depression or suicide. It is a huge field of hills, valleys, and pitfalls. All I can say is; "If you are having feelings you do not know how to deal with, it is okay, and there is always a way out!"

Now I am nearing the end of my book but certainly not the end of my life's adventures. Bob and I plan to retire in a few years, at which time we will travel and live our lives with all the joy we can. In closing I would like to just recap and hopefully give some suggestions to living a good life in point form.

A good life is lived to the fullest, often without a lot of financial success or notoriety. Money makes your life easier, not necessarily happier. You can have financial freedom and no happiness.

Remaining positive in the face of adversity...I decided to add this next section in the hope that some or all of you who read this book will be inspired. There will be times in your life when it's important to tap into a reserve you didn't know was there. I never like to "should" on anyone, but I will make strong suggestions and maybe even use the word "should" on occasion.

- My first advice is to look for your **inner passion**. What is it that keeps you centered? Know what gives you peace and concentrate on keeping peace close. You will be challenged in your faith, whatever that may be. Know that your faith will guide you.

- **Family** is extremely important. Do your best to remain positive in their presence and to maintain good relationships with them. If you are constantly down and blue, people, even family will eventually avoid being near you for their own self-preservation. Giving is important to maintaining family ties. Family relationships should never be one-sided. Family will always be family whether you like all the players or not. *"Family is not about blood. It's about who is willing to hold your hand when you need it most."* (www.informativeQuotes.com)

- **Learn to laugh at yourself.** We all do crazy things occasionally and being able to laugh along with everyone around you is very beneficial. A situation may be embarrassing at the time but you can laugh the second or third time you think about it. Setting your tone for the day with a smile in the morning is a good thing.

- You need to **remain positive** and take care of yourself. That may require distancing yourself from negativity and people who are depressed. Be supportive of others but do not allow them to drag you down.

Learn to laugh at yourself

- **Self-talk** is very important. Know that you have value and those concerns you may be stressing over will change, usually for the better. We believe what we tell ourselves. Tell yourself everything will work itself out; you are important; you are worthy of great things; you are loveable; the worrisome times too shall pass; you can be who you really are; the best is yet to come; you are strong; you can do this; your time is now. Each day tell yourself you are great. *"God didn't have time to make a nobody; he only made a somebody."* Mary Kay Ash

- **Gratitude**: If you aren't sure what to be grateful for, just find someone in a place that is worse than your own and be glad for where you are. This is a simple exercise. Just visit an emergency room or a care centre. Recently I attended our local hospital and found a lady in a wheelchair who was struggling trying to enter the building. She was very upset and obviously in pain. I offered my help and wheeled her inside. I noted she had no legs and was also losing her hands. Her fingers were gone almost back to the knuckles. I did not ask about her health but simply offered my help and she was obviously grateful. That same day I stopped to buy groceries. While parking my truck I noticed a motorcyclist pulling into a handicap spot. He also had no legs. My difficulties with my legs and mobility suddenly seemed very trivial. I must have needed a reminder.

An attitude of gratitude is easy to adopt when comparing your situation to someone whose difficulty exceeds your own. We all must be grateful for the good things in our lives, no matter how small. It is important to express gratitude, not only to ourselves, but to those who provide us with what we should be grateful for.

I read recently about a veteran who was in the Middle East on several separate tours of duty. He came away a wounded man with both severe physical and mental injuries including post-traumatic stress disorder. His challenges were far more than what I have faced and included the loss of his family. When I read his story, I wept. He saw more than any human person should and faced having to perform terrible acts in the name of war while defending his country. Yet he was able to overcome these challenges and lead a relatively normal life. What an inspiration he is for so many. This is the type of story that opens your eyes to some of the tragedies others face and yet they manage to carry on. Many Veterans deal with these types of challenges.

- **Dealing with grief** is essential. Grief has many faces and many stages. Know that you can talk to a professional and that doesn't mean you are mentally unstable. There may be times when you wonder if you will ever see a happier time. Especially if challenging events are constantly happening around you that affect your life in a profound way.

Watching your dreams die..."From the scattered dust of broken dreams rise the most amazing revelations and beginnings of new dreams and hope." – Lynda Drysdale

I have in my lifetime witnessed and experienced many broken dreams as well as goals that have not come to fruition. That does not mean they were not appropriate or fantastic. It only means they did not happen when I felt they should or my goals weren't really what I envisioned. Sometimes I just wasn't knowledgeable enough or didn't do the hard work required to achieve those goals. Anything that looks too easy usually isn't. Learning from my mistakes and broken dreams made me stronger. Bruised knees happen. We have to just pick ourselves up, dust ourselves off, and get on with our lives.

I cannot emphasize enough the importance of keeping a positive attitude. Some days you will have to reach a little farther to maintain your positive attitude. Life will throw you curve balls. Learning how to dodge them with positivity will help provide you with the courage to achieve your goals and live each day to the fullest.

From a very young age I learned to be positive and always knew I wanted more. When something did not turn out I just picked up the pieces and moved on. That's not to say I didn't fall on my knees and have my pity parties.

One thing I learned about pity parties though… people do not want to hear about them for very long. Think about it. How many people do you wish would just suck it up, get over it, and get on with life?

"Don't give up!

When things go wrong as they often will,

When the road you're trudging seems all uphill,

When funds are low and debts are high,

And you want to smile but you have to sigh,

When care is pressing you down a bit,

Rest if you must,

But don't you quit!" Unknown

Six very important rules I think are a must-have for happiness:

- Each day is a gift and we do with it what we choose. Make it the best day ever and learn something new every day.

"With the new day comes new strength and new thoughts." Eleanor Roosevelt

- Friends are presents even though occasionally you have to let them go. They may not be true friends or are "friends" for the wrong reasons. They may be a negative influence in your life. One of the best messages I have ever read:

"When you rise in life, your friends know who you are. When you fall, you know who your friends are!" (Unknown)

- Families are everything. This is where unconditional love comes into play. The saying blood is thicker than water is true. Even if your family members have done you wrong they are still family. Physical or mental abuse is not excusable but is forgivable and you must learn forgiveness in order to move on. That does not mean you need to ever keep that person close. It simply means that you can choose and move forward.

- Laugh often. Even in the face of adversity humor is healthy and can lighten the load. Someone once told me I could tell someone where to go with a smile on my face and they would enjoy the trip. Smile lines are something to be proud of.

- Love a lot. "Love can conquer all" is a phrase passed down through the ages. A human in love is unstoppable on so many levels. Happiness always includes "love." It can be the love of a child; the love of a pet (if you haven't a pet or never owned a pet, perhaps this is the time to go find one. They are so healing and their love is unconditional); love of one's self (which is of the utmost importance – just don't let it get out of hand. There is a difference between love and conceit); and of course the love of a project, or belief in a cause.

- Most if not all people, need the love of a human companion. Not everyone finds his or her true soul mate but most find happiness and a sense of well-being with someone special. Long relationships result from hard work but are very worth it. Do not give up on your partner when things get tough. There are so many situations that can be turned around to make a relationship stronger than it ever was before.

"Marriage is not 50-50; Divorce is 50-50.
Marriage has to be 100-100.
It isn't dividing everything in half, but giving everything you've got!" DaveWillis.org

Our children's future...I am concerned about the future of our children and grandchildren. We have come to a place where mothers are so very concerned about hurting their children's feelings. Not only are they worried about hurting the child's feelings but they have become over-protective to the point where children's expectations are excessive. My belief is that a mother hurts her child by not allowing a youngster to experience disappointments. Life is full of them and if a child does not learn how to deal with disappointment, living in the grown up world will be more than challenging.

We all get our feelings hurt. We cannot constantly protect our children from it. There are times when a parent must step up to defend a child, but when that child grows up and needs to fend for himself or herself, expecting others to give them what they want is not realistic.

It distresses me that schools are now playing sports where no one wins. This is not realistic either. In life there are winners and losers. We all must learn to lose gracefully and have the ability to bounce back to achieve success. We also have need to celebrate the wins in our lives, whether it is a team win or an individual win. Teaching a child to win or lose gracefully is more important to their growth than a moment of hurt feelings.

Children are very important in my life. I have always been concerned about their growth and encouragement. Teaching a child to cope with disappointment assists with his/her ability to take on new challenges without fear. I volunteered for many years in the Rodeo Queen programs in two provinces, working with young girls from age fourteen to twenty-four. Watching these young ladies grow and mature before my eyes was very rewarding. Helping them to deal with not being the successful contestant was part of that growth, and learning graciousness as a winner or 'loser' was equally important. There was always someone who came out on top and won the crown, but I tried to instill in my girls that just because you lose, you are not a loser. If you've given it all you had, you've gained from the experience.

"Love life. Engage in it. Give it all you've got. Love it with a passion, because life truly does give back, many times over, what you put into it." Maya Anjelou… (1928-2014)

Children also need to be taught the difference between **self-deserve** and **self-entitlement**. We all deserve to have a good life. We all deserve to be successful and have dreams come to fruition. However that requires dedication and work.

Too many people feel they are entitled to all they desire. Those who believe they are self-entitled sometimes find themselves in trouble when holding positions of power. Taking advantage to the detriment of others for your own gain doesn't bode well. This holds true for all ages, young to elderly, and in business or at play school. Politicians are a great example of someone in a position of power and some have left their post after abusing that power.

Another area of concern I have is the number of young women today that are involved in abusive relationships. Are we not raising our daughters to be independent and self-sufficient? The women of my generation were much more independent than the one before us, and it surprises me that our daughters are too often in danger from, or suffering the ill attentions of a man.

My next question is: Are we raising some of our sons to be demanding, selfish, self-centered controlling people who have no compassion for women? Their need for power can cloud what is right and wrong. Is this a self-entitled boy who feels self-deserving of everything he desires with nothing in return? For those of you who have sons here is a question for you. Would you want your daughter to date that man he is becoming?

I challenge young women who read this book and who may be in an unacceptable situation to know you have the power to change that situation. If you are indeed in a relationship that is detrimental to you, your family, or your safety, there must be a change. It will take bravery to move from a position of fear or control. There is so much help available. Do not be afraid to take the risk. It may mean removing yourself and your children to a safe place.

Many women do not even realize they are controlled. Recently I put together the following list for a young friend.

Controlling in the Name of Love...

Signs of Control:

- Unwavering claims of endless love, claiming you are the only one. He wants to be with you forever.

- Constantly talks about the future you will have together and dream casting

- Jealousy

- Wants to spend **all** his time with you

- Does not want to share you with anyone

- Takes you away from family (this may be distance or contact)

- Alienates you from friends

- Makes it difficult to see friends and family or go anywhere without him

- Says things like "I want to just crawl inside you and stay there"

- No stability – not in one place long enough for you to establish any relationships

- Has control of your money and/or vehicle so you must rely on him totally

- Brings property or pets into the relationship that would make it harder for you to leave

- Will use any number of excuses for you not to spend

time with family and or friends

- Makes you feel bad about leaving him alone for any length of time

Signs of Abuse:

- Restrains or hits you, and then says "I am so sorry, it will never happen again"
- Leaves marks on you as a brand or in areas where no one can see
- Does not want you to talk with any persons of the opposite sex
- Pulls you out of any grasp your family or friends may have
- Tries to make family and friends seem unworthy of your love or company
- Makes sure the only roots you have are him
- Makes it seem like the only stable thing in your life is him

The above are serious signs of an unhealthy relationship!

If you see any of these things happening in your relationship, you need to remove yourself from it. If there are threats you may need to seek shelter. Restraining orders often don't work but should be in place as well.

If you require help, call a family member or a friend you can trust, someone who will not contact him if you have to get away. It is never too late to get out.

There is help!

Having said all of this, there are many men in our society who are in abusive relationships as well. Men also do not need to be in situations where they are at risk mentally or physically. No one does.

In Summary...I wrote this book for my siblings, children and grandchildren, my mother, and for myself, but mostly for my husband who was my rock when I was very ill. Becoming suddenly ill is not what we bargain for in any relationship, particularly when we are relatively young and healthy. You never know what is in store for you. I was allergic to a very common medication, and it changed our lives forever.

We all must embrace our life. We never know when our life's journey may suddenly be altered or ended too soon. Too many people have left us with their song unsung.

Enjoying each day to the fullest, no matter your age, is very important. Not wasting time is equally important. "Enjoy each day and fill your cup with something wonderful," is my wish for all of the young people in my family.

My goal is to make at least one person smile every day! Make it yours too.

I decided writing this book may help someone reading it to find courage in battling some challenge in their life. I've had my share of challenges. I believe with each one I've become a stronger person. I also felt my family may want to read my story and know the personal struggles I've endured, many of which they may be unaware. I wish for my grandchildren to know me better when they read about my life. I wanted to leave something special for them in case we do not have the moments together for me to tell them.

"Nothing could have prepared me for this" was the title I chose because many of my experiences were life altering. As my story came alive on paper, it was very evident to me that my entire life was exactly what prepared me for what I faced. Had I not been prepared spiritually, mentally, and physically, I may not have come away from my challenges as well as I did.

"Every single thing that has happened in your life is preparing you for a moment that is yet to come." Unknown

At first I thought only to journal and keep it to myself. When I shared my story with Independent Mary Kay Sales Directors from across the country and realized the impact it had, I realized there was a need for me to write it down. I faced challenges beyond anything I could ever have imagined. I contemplated changing the title but was encouraged by friends to keep the one I initially chose. None of us think our lives can change so profoundly in such short order.

I have accumulated a wealth of experience and subsequently much wisdom to share. This has been a common sense look at my own life and life in general. Common sense is sadly lacking in our society today.

I hope you have enjoyed my stories, the sharing of my journey thus far. I also hope you had some laughs, maybe shed some tears, perhaps found a new sense of strength in yourself, a new perspective and some knowledge of what to do if faced with what appear to be insurmountable challenges.

I pray someone has a better day, a better week, and perhaps a better life.

"You cannot get through a single day without having an impact on the world around you. What you do makes a difference, and you have to decide what kind of difference you want to make." Jane Goodall

CPSIA information can be obtained at www.ICGtesting.com
Printed in the USA
LVOW11s0954030616

490860LV00002B/34/P